Developing Emotional Literacy with Teenage Boys

A Lucky Duck Book

Developing Emotional Literacy with Teenage Boys

Building Confidence, Self-esteem and Self-awareness

SAGE Publications

Developing Emotional Literacy with Teenage Boys

Building Confidence, Self-esteem and Self-awareness

Tina Rae
Lisa Pedersen

SAGE Publications
Los Angeles • London • New Delhi • Singapore

SAGE Publications Ltd
1 Oliver's Yard
55 City Road
London EC1Y 1SP

SAGE Publications Inc.
2455 Teller Road
Thousand Oaks, California 91320

SAGE Publications India Pvt. Ltd.
B 1/I 1 Mohan Cooperative Industrial Area
Mathura Road, Post Bag 7
New Delhi 110 044

SAGE Publications Asia-Pacific Pte Ltd
33 Pekin Street #02-01
Far East Square
Singapore 048763

www.luckyduck.co.uk

Library of Congress Control Number: 2006932349

British Library Cataloguing in Publication data

A Catalogue record for this book is available from the British Library

ISBN 978-1-4129-3032-1

Typeset by C&M Digitals (P) Ltd, Chennai, India
Printed in India by Replika Press Pvt. Ltd.
Printed on paper from sustainable resources.

Contents

How to Use the CD-ROM

The CD-ROM contains a PDF file labelled 'Activity Sheets pdf' which consists of worksheets for each session in the resource. You will need Acrobat Reader version 3 or higher to view and print these pages.

The document is set up to print to A4 but you can enlarge the pages to A3 by increasing the output percentage at the point of printing using the page set-up settings for your printer.

Introduction and Rationale

This resource introduces a programme, called 'Boys' World', to support high school boys in developing their confidence, self-esteem and self-awareness. A major focus is also placed upon the development of emotional literacy and the ways in which boys can effectively contribute to peer support structures and mechanisms which aid the inclusion of all boys in both the social and the school arenas. It was originally developed for, and delivered to, a group of boys within the context of a Pupil Referral Unit. However, given that the issues and the content covered are obviously pertinent to all boys, we have compiled the 12 sessions into a programme, which can be delivered to both smaller groups and whole classes of boys at high school level.

The Emotional Mis-education of Boys

Much of the current literature on boys' development reveals that the definition of masculinity within our westernised culture is extremely narrow. Metaphorically speaking, it places boys inside a box that limits their emotional and relational development. Psychologists describe how healthy psychological development has been typically marked by progressive acquisition and integration of new skills and qualities. In contrast to this, the traditional male socialisation described by Terrence Real (1997) reflects a process of disconnection marked by successive 'disavowing' and loss of qualities essential to boys' emotional and psychological well-being.

It would appear that within our culture there exists a set of unique stressors which continue to propel today's young males down a very troubled path. Daniel Kindlon and Michael Thompson (1999) describe the emotional illiteracy of boys that develops from a so-called disavowing process and its bearing on both the personal and the social problems that boys experience in schools. The lack of emotional connection is often mixed with a sense of privilege, power and entitlement that also stems from traditional masculine ideals. Therefore, it is not surprising that such factors may influence boys to behave in disrespectful and antisocial ways towards their teachers and their peers.

For many boys it seems that schools are in a sense 'anti-boy'. When entering Key Stages 1/2, boys will find a curriculum which emphasises the acquisition of basic literacy skills, i.e. reading and writing, and this, to some extent, can restrict their activities. Boys are generally far more active and slower to read than girls and teachers will often discipline boys more harshly than they would the girls within the classroom context. Consequently, sensitivity is not modelled to the boys so we would argue that they do not learn it. Alongside this anti-boy school culture, it would seem that fathers and male carers tend to demand that their sons act tough. Mothers and female carers also tend to expect boys to be strong and protective. Furthermore, their peer group will often enforce the rule that a boy does not cry or show his emotions. Boys are taught not to be 'sissies' and at the same time, are chastised for being insensitive. It is not surprising that boys become confused when they are hearing such different messages, i.e. to embrace an androgynous sex while not becoming too feminine. Also, for many boys, experiences of losing early friends as they enter into adolescence can cause enormous amounts of stress. For many teenage boys the distrust of other boys replaces intimate same sex friendships. Boys are also bombarded with images in the media which have, over time, become more hyper-masculine. Emotionless killing machines such as Sylvester Stallone, for example, have supplanted the strong yet milder heroes like Roy Rogers. Boys are presented with scenarios in which they must learn to hide behind a mask of bravado. Boys are also often victims of ruthless jeering, insults and cussing. Many of them find that words do not stop the taunting, but physical violence and aggression do. It seems that anger is the only emotion that earns them respect.

James Gabarino (1999) describes how the symptoms of boys' growing dissatisfaction, which had been previously ignored, have been steadily building. Rising numbers of boys are prescribed the drug Ritalin for Attention Deficit Hyperactivity Disorder (ADHD), possibly often legitimately. However, in many cases it is over-prescribed to curb acting-out behaviours. It is also evident that boys' academic performance has declined within the last decade while girls' achievements have risen. The same pattern is true for attendance within further education and boys are far more likely than girls to hurt or kill themselves or each other.

The kind of psychological detachment and rigidly defined behaviour for boys that we have described frequently leads to violent or aggressive acts. In his study on violence, James Gilligan (1999) observes that boys and men tend to be preoccupied with the issue of weak versus strong and that this focus may frequently be at the root of aggressive and violent behaviours, alongside expressions of power and personal interactions. As he states, 'it's not too difficult to see how quickly that preoccupation with weakness evolves into a predisposition to prove one's strength by means of violence, particularly if the child does not have non-violent means available to show that he is strong'. That said it is not surprising that 80% of the students diagnosed with social and emotional difficulties in schools are boys while 71% of all school suspensions also involve boys.

A Man's World?

Statistics on men's health, happiness and survival clearly show that the old adage 'it's a man's world' is simply a lie. Being a boy or a man in the early twenty-first century is clearly not an easy option for the following reasons:

- ▸ Men on average live for six years less than women do.
- ▸ Men routinely fail at close relationships: 40% of marriages break down and divorces are initiated by the women in 4 out of 5 cases.
- ▸ 90% of convicted acts of violence will be carried out by men and 70% of the victims will be male.
- ▸ In school around 90% of children with behavioural problems and 80% of children with learning problems are boys.
- ▸ 1 in 7 boys will experience sexual assault by an adult or older child by the age of 18.
- ▸ Men comprise over 90% of inmates in prison and make up 74% of the unemployed.
- ▸ The leading cause of death among men aged between 12 and 60 is through self-inflicted means. In 1993 Australian Bureau of Statistics (ABS) figures, suicide accounted for 1 in 38 male deaths overall (Biddulph, 1995).

Suicide Rates among Young Men

Suicide rates among young men in the United Kingdom rose significantly during the 1980s and the early 1990s. This has led to a significant amount of political attention being drawn to this topic and rightly so, given that suicide rates in England and Wales of young men between the ages of 15 and 24 rose by approximately 60% from 1981 to 1999. This led the government to set a goal in 1991 (Health of the Nation Strategy Document) to reduce the rates of these suicides by 15% by the end of the century. The rate has been reduced from approximately 16 in 100,000 in 1990 to 12 in 100,000 in 2000.

In order to further support the government's health strategy in this area, a specific 'National Suicide Prevention Strategy for England' was issued in 2002. This strategy has six identified objectives, including: reducing risk in key high-risk groups, e.g. men; promoting mental health and well-being in the wider population; and reducing the availability and lethal nature of suicide methods. It is still the case, however, that young men are far more likely to commit suicide than young women. The risk factors have been clearly documented between both primary and secondary factors. Obviously no one young person would experience all of the factors but they are likely to experience a significant combination. This kind of combination could then lead to an increased risk of suicide. Primary factors include the following:

▶ Alcohol and drug abuse.

▶ A sense of real hopelessness concerning the future.

▶ Serious depression.

▶ A previous attempted suicide or some form of psychiatric disorder.

Secondary risk factors include:

▶ Severe dent to self-esteem which may lead to a sense of guilt or shame.

▶ A recent loss or bereavement.

▶ A family history of suicide.

▶ Experiencing a friend or significant adult committing suicide.

Most significant for us in developing this particular project were the risk factors related to lack of self-esteem leading to a sense of guilt or shame. In our culture boys generally are led to believe that in order to be manly they must stay 'on top of their feelings'. They consequently live in psychological conflict because they are attempting to control feelings that may be too powerful or too complex to be controlled. As Kindlon and Thompson (1999) state, 'the results can be deadly: combined depression and its shame, emotional illiteracy, and the impulsivity so common among boys: mix in access to weapons and a familiarity with violence, real or through the media – and you have recipe for suicide'. Clearly not every boy who confronts emotional hardship will develop severe depression. Whether or not depression is biological or situational in origin, the recovery from it is far more difficult for boys who, according to Kindlon and Thompson, have been 'trained away from emotional interaction and steered instead towards emotional silence and stoicism' (1999, p. 167).

Combating Emotional Illiteracy

According to Biddulph (1995) men's difficulties are primarily with isolation. The prisons from which they must escape are:

▶ Loneliness.

▶ Compulsive competition.

▶ Lifelong emotional timidity.

Consequently, a significant aim of this programme is to promote the boys' levels of emotional literacy in order to also foster and protect their mental health. The latter is key given that, 'since the 1940s the number of children experiencing mental ill health has increased to 1 in 5' (The Big Picture Report, 1999). This Mental Health Foundation report also stated that:

mental health problems in children and young people will continue to increase unless there is a coherent and holistic programme implemented to develop the emotional and mental health of our children. ... Emotionally literate children are less likely to experience mental health problems and, if they develop them, are less likely to suffer long term. Emotional literacy is derived from a combination of parents, schools and wider social networks.

Daniel Goleman (1995) defines emotional literacy as 'the capacity for recognising our own feelings and those of others, for motivating ourselves and for managing emotions within ourselves and in our relationships'. Consequently, this programme attempts to begin to promote boys' emotional literacy and mental health within the educational context while also promoting the notion of emotional learning as an important lifelong goal in every sphere.

According to Suzy Orbach emotional literacy is achieved by registering emotions, recognising our emotions, querying them for validity and then being able to put them aside after having experienced them (Improving Mental Health for Young People Conference, October 2000). The essential aim of this programme is therefore to ensure that boys have access to experiences which encourage them to develop the skills of emotional literacy within the solution-focused forum, which rejects the notion of compulsive competition. We are not attempting in any sense to negate differences but rather to validate students' own experiences and to encourage them to develop the motivation, resilience and trust with which to become be emotionally successful and stable human beings.

Objectives

The main objectives of this 12-session programme are to:

▸ Encourage students to become more aware of the importance of supporting each other and the benefits of forming strong and positive links with other males.

▸ Develop students' understanding of emotional literacy and the importance of being aware of their feelings and being able to manage them effectively.

▸ Ensure that students understand the importance of self-motivation and positive thinking.

▸ Raise students' self-esteem and levels of confidence.

▸ Encourage students to develop the ability to make their own decisions in life.

▸ Encourage students to become more aware and questioning of the impact that the media has on the way that they behave and the way in which they see themselves.

▸ Enable students to further develop and appreciate the perspectives of others – to empathise.

▸ Further develop students' awareness of gender differences and the way in which stereotypes can be imposed and built in to the way in which we behave towards each other.

▸ Develop students' awareness of what it is to be healthy and the way in which risky behaviours can mitigate against both mental and physical well-being.

▸ Encourage students to develop problem-solving skills within a solution-focused framework.

▸ Develop students' tolerance of difference and rejection of stereotypes.

▸ Raise awareness of the importance of relationships and the ways in which our behaviour can mitigate against maintaining positive relationships.

- Further develop the facilitator's awareness and understanding of a range of strategies to effectively manage one's self and one's emotions.

- Encourage facilitators and support staff to adopt a consistent approach towards developing students' emotional literacy, social skills and self-esteem.

- Further encourage facilitators to review the current policy and practice in terms of managing the emotional, social and behavioural needs of students in their care.

- Further develop healthy initiatives and programmes which promote inclusive practice for those students who present as being most at risk.

- Encourage facilitators to reflect further upon how the school and curriculum are structured so as to ensure the inclusion of boys, i.e. that the curriculum and adults who teach it model positive images of the male sex and that the curriculum is suitably differentiated to ensure the inclusion of boys within all subject areas.

- Further develop and encourage facilitators' awareness of the need to provide adequate pastoral support for boys within Key Stages 3 and 4, e.g. the use of mentors.

The success of this programme will clearly depend upon how closely these objectives are followed and achieved.

The Structure of the Programme

The Programme is divided into 12 sessions. Each session includes an Introduction in which the main aims are recorded and discussed. A similar format is then adhered to which includes a brainstorming activity, a 'quick' activity/icebreaker, Circle Talk, A Problem Scenario, a range of Activity Sheets for Students to complete and a final Plenary session. The sessions are arranged in the following sequence:

Session 1: Identity

Session 2: Appearance

Session 3: Girlfriends

Session 4: Friendships

Session 5: Sex

Session 6: Problem Solving

Session 7: Talking about Feelings

Session 8: Drugs Awareness

Session 9: Tolerance

Session 10: Crime and Punishment

Session 11: Future Goals

Session 12: Evaluation

The Structure of the Sessions

The sessions generally follow a similar structure as follows.

Introduction

The main aims of the session are recorded by the facilitator on a flip-chart or whiteboard and these are discussed with the students at the outset. A list of key words is brainstormed and also recorded.

Brainstorm

Students are asked to brainstorm in order to identify all the words or phrases that they can which relate to this particular topic. A completed brainstorm is provided for facilitators in order to prompt thinking and provide relevant ideas.

Quick Activity

A range of quick activities or icebreakers are used to break down barriers and create a comfortable and unthreatening context in which students can begin to form positive relationships and relax in order to subsequently engage in the activities presented to them.

Circle Talk

The circle talk element of the session encourages students to begin to articulate ideas and feelings. A series of questions are presented which relate specifically to the topic being introduced. A Circle Time approach is adopted in which students adhere to rules regarding turn-taking and respect for each other's views. The group rules which are identified and agreed by students in the first session will clearly be reinforced in each of the subsequent circle talk sessions.

Problem Scenario

The students are presented with a problem scenario in which a boy is experiencing a difficulty or problem. They are then asked to consider a series of questions which focus on the ways in which the boy might find a solution to the dilemma that he is currently facing and how he might deal more effectively with the problem.

Central to this activity is the need to ensure that all boys feel able to participate. There is consequently no recording here. The activity is entirely verbal. The key aim is clearly to encourage boys to articulate thoughts and feelings. Given that they are not being identified as personally experiencing this problem, we hope that students will feel more inclined to discuss the feelings that the character in each of the scenarios may be experiencing and to offer solutions, i.e. developing empathy en route.

A 'solution focused' (Rhodes and Ajmal, 1995) sheet is provided for each of the scenarios and students are asked to identify the problem and to explore how the central character feels. They are then asked to identify how he might feel if things were different or better: if a miracle happened and the problem went away, how would the character feel? They are finally asked to identify three things that the character in the scenario can do now in order to remove the problem from his life.

These scenarios will hopefully reflect some of the problems and pressures that the boys are currently experiencing. This format should also allow them to develop their skills particularly in the areas of empathy and problem solving, which can then be transferred into their own real-life experiences and problems.

Activity Sheets

In order to further clarify and reinforce specific skills and concepts, the students are presented with a series of activity sheets. These can require students to either work individually, in pairs or in smaller groups. The aim of these activities is generally to promote the development of personal skills and particularly to foster students' ability to cooperate and work effectively as a member of a group. What is also important here is the fact that the majority of these activities demand very little recording. When trialling this programme within the context of a Pupil Referral Unit, we were obviously dealing with many boys whose literacy skills were not all that highly developed. There were also issues around attention and motivation. Consequently, asking these boys to adopt a learning style which would reinforce any difficulties or problems they might be encountering would not have been productive. For many young men at this stage, the main aim of any such programme should be to focus on developing their ability to express their feelings, thoughts and ideas verbally – opportunities which many boys do not have access to within the social, or possibly within their own school, context.

Plenary

During the final part of each session, the brainstorming approach will again be utilised in order to elicit the students' views of the session. Not only is this an opportunity to summarise the skills and concepts covered, but it is also important to encourage the students to reflect upon the usefulness of the tasks, and begin to identify ways in which they might be able to further develop their own skills. A list of key questions is provided in order to promote thinking and to encourage participation in this part of the session.

Notes for Facilitators

The sessions can be used in a variety of ways either within a small group context or within the whole class. Although the programme has been developed within the context of a Pupil Referral Unit and subsequently used with smaller groups of students, it would be feasible to utilise these resources within the larger group and adapt them as appropriate for specific groups of students.

It may be helpful, however, to consider and take into account the fact that these resources have been developed to specifically target the needs of boys. Although some of the resources could be adapted for use in mixed gender groups, it should be noted that they are intended to provide a programme that can be delivered to boys within the context of a safe and nurturing group in which they can express their feelings, views and ideas without embarrassment or fear (i.e. feelings that adolescent boys may well experience if observed by adolescent girls). It is not felt that the gender of the facilitator is particularly important as it is assumed that he/she will have the requisite skills in managing this type of group work. However, it may be helpful, in a mixed gender school, to consider the possibility of running two groups simultaneously (i.e. one for boys and one for girls).

When initially trialling this programme, both the Special Educational Needs Coordinator (SENCO) and the Educational Psychologist were allocated to the target group in order to deliver each of these sessions, and to provide ongoing weekly mentoring support with individual students. However, it does not necessarily follow that similar arrangements should, or could, be made in other contexts. The allocation of resources and attempts to work in such a multi-disciplinary way clearly need to be appropriate to each context. However, it is important to ensure that those delivering this programme have some interest in both emotional literacy and social and behavioural skills themselves, and that they are able to function within an emotionally literate and supportive environment. It is also useful if facilitators have had some experience of managing groups and some understanding of group processes.

Focus on Boys: Some Useful Tips

Alongside experience of managing groups and understanding how these may and may not function effectively, it is also useful for facilitators to specifically consider how they initially approach groups of young men and perhaps agree both their philosophy and a range of useful strategies and approaches. The latter is particularly important when the individuals being targeted present as disaffected or disengaged with the learning culture. Clearly, the facilitators will be aware of positive behaviour management strategies, but when first approaching a group of less engaged young men, the task can appear somewhat daunting. When initially delivering this programme within the Pupil Referral Unit context, we agreed a range of strategies and approaches. Many of these may appear obvious to the more experienced professional, but we felt that it might be useful to present them as a list of 'useful tips' for working with young men. It may be useful for facilitators to discuss the list prior to delivering the course, during the course (as a direct result of delivering specific activities) and subsequent to completion of the course. Our list was as follows:

▸ Always explain 'why' a task is being done and what the purpose of the activity really is. For example, we need to become emotionally literate in order to be successful in our relationships and future jobs, etc. There is a reason for doing this work.

▸ Ensure that the students are not targeted individually to 'give their views, thoughts or feelings' in front of the group. When they are clearly not ready to do so, don't push them.

▸ Use examples of other men's or boys' experiences rather than asking directly 'What did you do when ...?' This can come across as confrontational to a young man who is experiencing low levels of confidence and self-esteem. Focusing on others' experiences feels 'safer' and can encourage the students to relate back to personal experiences at a later stage.

▸ Always ask for students' thoughts and opinions and don't judge them. They need to know that their views are valid (no matter how sexist or inappropriate they may appear).

▸ Always model the behaviour you wish to see and join in the activities. It is really important that embarrassment is always reduced to a minimum. If the facilitator is always first to 'have a go' and willing to share his/her own experiences, this can help to deflect difficult emotions and alleviate any stress. However, the facilitator will need to be very clear as to the extent he/she wishes to disclose more personal information and the usefulness or otherwise of adopting such a strategy.

▸ Use humour to deflect difficult situations and/or emotions but never use it as a put-down. This is entirely unproductive.

▸ Always use praise to reinforce the boys' contributions and appropriate behaviours and 'catch them' as frequently as possible 'doing the right thing'. It is vital to highlight the positives and, as far as possible, ignore the negatives.

▸ Move on quickly to the next activity or another point in the structured conversation at the first hint of any embarrassment. Never insist on each student making a contribution but simply praise those who do and thank them every time.

▸ Always allow time for talking. This is particularly important. Boys need time to think and respond and you may often have to allow them to talk 'round' a topic for some time before they feel able to address a specific point or key issue.

- Ensure that activities are mainly practical and that they are presented so as to incorporate a range of learning styles. Providing visual and kinaesthetic prompts and activities are vital for boys who exhibit more limited concentration sparks. Activities should always, to some extent, be specific and time limited.

Most important, in our view, is probably the first item in this list: why are we doing this? Why do we need to learn these skills? We would always emphasise not only the need to protect and foster emotional well-being but also the 'real world' value and importance of developing the skills of emotional literacy. These are the skills that they will need in the real world if they are to work effectively in teams, solving problems and communicating appropriately with work colleagues. These are the life skills that will ensure they are successful in both work and personal relationships and that they can remain resilient and motivated when they do experience problems and setbacks.

Hartley-Brewer's (2001) rationale is probably most apt:

> Boys must learn how to be in touch with their own and others' feelings and perceptions because technological progress and greater global competition are creating jobs that require creative team work, collective problem-solving, constant communication and joint approaches to risk.

We do hope that these 'tips' are of use, particularly to the facilitator who may have less experience of working with young men who may present as somewhat disaffected and unwilling to engage. In order to further support implementation of the programme, we have included 'Tips' throughout each of the subsequent session plans. These are designed to help the facilitator pre-empt and avoid difficulties (mainly those we have experienced ourselves) and to support a smoother and more confident delivery.

Notes on Aspects of the Sessions

It is helpful to have the aims of each session written up on the flip-chart prior to the start of the session, alongside any key words pertinent to the topic being covered. These can be added to by the students within an initial brainstorming activity.

Brainstorm

Students are then asked to brainstorm all the words or phrases that they can which relate to the particular topic of the session. The facilitator can record students' answers on a flip-chart before asking them to transfer the words or phrases onto the 'Key Words Brainstorm' sheet provided. Alternatively, students could take time to work on the sheets individually, but answers should be discussed as a group at some point. Facilitators can use the completed brainstorm in order to prompt thinking and provide relevant ideas.

Quick Activity

Quick activities are icebreaker activities which usually consist of a quick game. The idea here is to break down any barriers and create a positive climate for the remainder of the session.

In the introductory session, the students initially agree to group rules and it is vital that an appropriate amount of time is allocated for this aspect of the course so as to ensure ownership of the rules. This will also allow each student to then adhere to the rules in subsequent sessions. Reinforcing group rules prior to clarifying the aims of each session is also helpful.

Circle Talk

The circle talk aspect of each session adopts the Circle Time approach. It is important that this process is described clearly to students and that facilitators are fully aware of this process and how to use it to the greatest effect. As stated previously, agreeing the group rules prior to any Circle Time is also clearly essential.

Problem Scenario

In order to introduce each of the scenarios it may be helpful for the facilitator to read through the problem scenarios to the students. This reduces any pressure on boys who have difficulties in the area of literacy skills development. It may also be useful for the facilitators to participate in making use of the problem-solving framework provided and to share their ideas with the boys. Role modelling the process and presenting their own ideas in the framework in a democratic way, i.e. valuing both students' and facilitators' views, feelings, thoughts and ideas, is one way of doing this.

Activity Sheets

The facilitator can then introduce the activity sheets that aim to both clarify and reinforce the specific topic introduced within the session. The sheets are designed to require minimal amounts of recording such as drawing, writing or discussing. They can be stored in individual folders, which the students can make up at the start of the programme. These can be designed individually and we strongly encourage facilitators to allow some additional time for this, as good presentation of the work involved will invariably raise the profile of the group and its focus.

It will, of course, be important to take notice of students whose recording skills are under-developed in order to provide any additional peer or adult support during these activities. However, we would anticipate that the facilitator will be skilled in differentiation and therefore able to ensure access for all students regardless of their level of ability. We would also recommend that, throughout each of the sessions, the facilitator emphasises and promotes the notion of peer support, given that one of the aims of the project is to raise boys' awareness of the importance of friendship. This, in turn, can foster mental and emotional well-being and reduce their isolation in both the home and the school context.

Plenary

This part of the session encourages the students to feed back their ideas and responses on the activity sheets and to also focus on the main elements covered in the session. It would be helpful for the facilitator to briefly summarise the main concepts covered and to record any responses from the students on the flip-chart or whiteboard. This will allow for highlighting and validating experiences, ideas and feelings that may be common to the majority of students while also reinforcing any useful or not so useful strategies. It will also encourage students to highlight any difficulties or concerns that they may have had and to further self-reflect upon their own skills and the best way of moving forward.

Looking Forward

As with all such programmes, it will be important to ensure that an appropriate level of support is provided for individual students who require it once the sessions have been completed. It may be helpful to continue to provide some weekly tutorial support for targeted individuals should they request it. It will also be helpful to encourage the boys to continue with problem-solving group work, providing a support network for each other which can also be further supported by other adults within the school context.

We would hope that, in the longer term, school staff will become more aware of the need to promote the self-esteem and emotional literacy of boys in particular, and of the need to guard against stereotyping boys and combating their social and emotional isolation which can lead to the aggressive behaviours and mental ill health that we wish to reduce. Hopefully, maintaining and fostering the kind of empathic and solution-focused problem solving highlighted within these sessions will go some way to achieving such a goal.

We are living at an important and fruitful moment now, for it is clear to men that the images of adult manhood given by popular culture are worn out; and man can no longer depend on them. By the time a man is 35, he knows that the images of the right man, the tough man, the true man, which he received in high school, do not work in life. Such a man is open to new visions of what a man is or could be. (Robert Bly, quoted in Biddulph, 1995, p. 9)

References

Biddulph, S. (1995) *Manhood: An Action Plan for Changing Men's Lives,* Sydney: Finch Publishing.

Biddulph, S. (1997) *Raising Boys: Why Boys Are Different – and How to Help Them Become Happy and Well-balanced Men*, London: Thorsons.

Coleman, J. (2004) *Teenage Suicide and Self-harm – A Training Pack for Professionals*, Brighton: Trust for the Study of Adolescence.

Department of Health (2001) *Making It Happen: A Guide to Delivering Mental Health Promotion*, London: Department of Health Publications.

Equal Opportunities Commission (EOC) and Office for Standards in Education (Ofsted) (1996) *The Gender Divide: Performance Differences between Boys and Girls at School*, London: HMSO.

Gabarino, M. (1999) *Lost Boys: Why Our Sons Turn Violent and How We Can Save Them*, New York: Free Press.

Gilligan, J. (1999) *Boys to Men: Questions of Violence*, www.edletter.org/past/issues/1999-ja/forum.shtml questions.

Goleman, D. (1995) *Emotional Intelligence: Why It Can Matter More Than IQ*, New York: Bantam Books.

Harris, I. M. (1995) *Messages Men Hear: Constructing Masculinities*, London: Taylor & Francis.

Hartley-Brewer, E. (2001) *Raising Confident Boys*, Cambridge, MA: Dalapo Press.

Kindlon, D. and Thompson, M. (1999) *Raising Cain: Protecting the Emotional Life of Boys*, London: Penguin books.

Marris, B. and Rae, T. (2004) *Escape from Exclusion*, London: Lucky Duck Publishing.

Rae, T. (2004) *Emotional Survival: An Emotional Literacy Programme for High School Students*, London: Lucky Duck Publishing.

Rae, T., Nelson, L. and Pederson, L. (2005) *Developing Emotional Literacy with Teenage Girls: Building Confidence, Self-esteem and Self-respect*, London: Lucky Duck Publishing.

Real, T. (1997) *I Don't Want to Talk About It: Overcoming the Secret Legacy of Male Depression*, New York: Scribner.

Rhodes, J. and Ajmal, Y. (1995) *Solution Focused Thinking in Schools*, London: Brief Therapy Publications.

Salisbury, J. and Riddell, S. (2000) *Gender, Policy and Educational Change: Shifting agendas in the UK and Europe*, Abingdon: Routledge.

Smith, C. (2004a) *Circle Time for Adolescents*, London: Lucky Duck Publishing.

Smith, C. (2004b) *Concluding Circle Time with Secondary Students*, London: Lucky Duck Publishing.

Sukhandan, L., Lee, B. and Kelleher, S. (2000) *An Investigation into Gender Differences in Achievement*, London: NFER.

The Big Picture Report (1999) by the Mental Health Foundation, February.

Websites for Young Men

The following is a list of websites that may be helpful for the facilitator to refer to during the sessions. These can be recommended to the young men as and when it is necessary. Some young men may feel more comfortable seeking out advice and information on their own if they are uncomfortable discussing it in a group.

Brook Education

www.brook.org.uk

Provides sexual health and relationships advice and information. Users can play a fun sexually transmitted infections (STIs) game.

Childline

www.childline.org.uk

National helpline: 0800 1111. Open 24 hours a day, 365 days a year.

This service provides a free, confidential telephone counselling service for children or young people with any problem. Information for children and young people, as well as professionals, is also available via the website.

Getting it on

www.gettingiton.org.uk/index.aspx

An interactive site providing information on sexual health, contraception and pregnancy.

Like it is

www.likeitis.org.uk

Designed for young people, this website provides honest information about all aspects of sex education and teenage life.

Marie Stopes

www.mariestopes.org.uk

Telephone: 0845 300 8090

An information resource used by people of all ages, which provides online sexual health information and advice on issues such as abortion, pregnancy and STIs.

Sexwise

www.ruthinking.co.uk

Confidential advice line for young people: 0800 28 29 30 Provides information on sexual health for young people. The site will provide details of the nearest STI clinic when a post code is provided.

Teenage Health Freak

www.teenagehealthfreak.org/homepage/index.asp

Comprehensive website for teenagers, including facility to email questions, on a wide range of medical and sexual issues.

The Site

www.thesite.org/

The user can search for advice centres that deal with specific issues including: general health, drugs, alcohol, sexuality and sexual health.

There4me

www.there4me.com

Confidential online advice for teenagers, including 'real time' talk with an NSPCC adviser. Subjects covered range from bullying, relationships, drugs and exams.

Young Minds

www.youngminds.org.uk

Comprehensive website for teenagers, including facility to email questions, on a wide range of medical and sexual issues.

Session 1

Identity

The facilitator can outline the main aims of this session as follows:

- For students to become aware of the objectives and main themes that will be examined in the sessions.

- For students to work together to agree on a set of ground rules for the course.

- For students and facilitator(s) to learn more about themselves and each other in order to begin to build more trusting relationships with one another.

In this initial session it will also be important for the facilitator to clarify the aims of the project as a whole. As this is the first session in the programme, it may be helpful to allocate additional time to cover the activities and ensure that group rules are given due attention and thought.

The facilitator may wish to make use of the whiteboard or flip-chart in order to highlight the main objectives of the course as follows. Within the framework of the programme the students will be encouraged to:

- Create a sense of trust and confidence in each other.

- Build up new friendships and consolidate their existing ones.

- Create a sense of belonging to a group.

- Develop their self-esteem and self-confidence.

- Extend their social skills in speaking and listening.

- Develop a positive attitude and maintain motivation.

- Further develop empathy for others.

- Promote understanding and tolerance, developing positive behaviours and the ability to self-reflect and modify behaviours.

- Develop assertiveness skills.

- Increase their level of emotional literacy, particularly the ability to identify and express feelings and the consequences of feelings and behaviours.

- Understand the nature of boyhood and manhood and be able to self-reflect on their own perspectives, thoughts and feelings about their gender.

- Develop problem-solving skills within a solution-focused context.

- Become more aware of the nature of friendship and the importance of developing healthy ones.

The students will be asked to contribute to the series of 12 sessions in order to develop their own skills and competencies, and to also learn how to work effectively as part of a solution-focused problem-solving group.

The topics to be covered will include the following:

- Awareness of identity.

- Appearance and its link to self-esteem.

- Relationships.
- Friendships and peer pressure.
- Safe and unsafe sex.
- Problem solving.
- Talking about feelings.
- Drugs awareness.
- Tolerance.
- Crime and punishment.
- Developing future goals.
- Evaluating progress.

The facilitator may wish to also highlight the structure of subsequent sessions in which the boys will be asked to consider a range of problems that they themselves may have experienced. They will be asked to work together in solving these problems via solution-focused approaches. Sessions will follow a similar pattern as follows:

- A short introduction.
- Brainstorm.
- Quick activity.
- Circle talk.
- Problem scenario.
- Activity sheets.
- Plenary.

This initial session largely follows the above sequence but incorporates the setting of group rules so as to ensure the inclusion and safety of all students within subsequent sessions.

Introduction

Students are asked to focus on the following question:

What factors influence our identity?

Students can record their views on the blank Key Words Brainstorm sheet provided, or the facilitator may wish to record students' views on a whiteboard or flip-chart.

> ## Tip
>
> **The facilitator can model the initial responses in order to avoid any embarrassment and prompt the students' thinking (see the Facilitator's Notes for some suggestions). Don't expect all the students to feel willing or able to contribute the first or second time.**

Brainstorm

Students are asked to brainstorm and to identify all the words and phrases that they can relate to this topic. The facilitator can once again provide initial prompts if necessary. Ideas can be recorded on the blank Key Words Brainstorm sheet provided, or the facilitator may wish to scribe the students' suggestions on a whiteboard of flip-chart.

Quick Activity

Students are asked to work in pairs. The facilitator describes the task and explains to the students that this is a timed activity. They have two minutes to identify the three biggest influences on their identities. Ideas can be recorded on the Quick Activity sheet provided. It may be helpful to provide the students with an example as follows:

Three biggest influences on my identity are:

1. People in the media who are famous like David Beckham.
2. Music, music videos and fashion clothes.
3. Sports, sports wear and sports personalities.

Tip

Try to pair students so as to ensure one can 'take the lead' and model responses and support the other as far as possible.

Circle Talk

In this initial circle talk activity the students introduce themselves in turn, identifying three main points about themselves that they would like the others to know. For example:

I've got a sense of humour.
I've got a pet snake.
I've got three older sisters.

This can then be further extended through a paired activity in which students are asked to question each other for two minutes in order to find out as many facts as possible about each other. These facts can then be fed back to the group via each of the partners in turn.

It can also be a useful activity to ask each of the boys in turn around the circle what they think they will learn from this course. The facilitator may wish to focus on the following three key questions:

- ▸ What do I like about being a boy?

- ▸ What don't I like about being a boy?

- ▸ What is hard or easy about being a boy?

Group Rules

The group rules for these sessions need to be agreed and owned by all the students involved and should be reinforced at the beginning of each subsequent session. The facilitator can explain that the rules should be formulated in order to ensure the safety of every member of the group and to protect their self-esteem throughout the duration of the course. Students can be asked to contribute initially via a brainstorming process in order to ensure that group rules are owned by all involved. These rules may include the following:

▶ Everyone needs to listen to each other.

▶ Everyone needs to take turns.

▶ Everyone needs to respect each other's space and ideas.

▶ Everyone has the right to pass.

▶ Everyone in the group needs to try to give ideas and offer solutions.

▶ Everyone needs to use their imagination.

▶ Everyone must be careful not to criticise others' ideas but to build upon them.

▶ Everyone must agree what is talked about in these sessions, will stay in the sessions, and will not be discussed with people outside the group.

For future sessions, the group rules can be recorded on the sheet provided. The facilitator may wish to enlarge this to A3 size in order to record students' ideas during the session. However, it may also be helpful for each student in the group to have an A4 copy of the format so as to record the rules for themselves and file these in the individual folders or course books as appropriate. These books can be made up prior to the start of the course or during this first session as time allows.

Problem Scenario

The students are presented with the problem scenario entitled 'Identity'. In this scenario, Joel is experiencing some difficulties in terms of his own identity. He is mixed race with a Jamaican mother and a White British father. He finds it difficult to fit in with the white students and he struggles to do so with the black students. His father also doesn't like him going around with the 'black crowd' whom he regards as gangsters.

The facilitator can read the problem scenario to the students. Alternatively, students may wish to read the text by themselves or nominate another student to read it aloud. They can then make use of the Solution-focused Problem-solving Format in order to identify a way forward for Joel. This involves identifying how Joel feels, clarifying the problem and how Joel might behave if the problem were removed, i.e. the miracle question idea. They are finally asked to identify three things that Joel could do now in order to remove the problem from his life.

Activity Sheets

Activity 1 – This Is Me

This activity asks each student to identify different aspects of themselves, e.g. appearance, likes, dislikes, religion, hobbies, etc. They are then asked to consider, via discussion, whether or not they are similar to other members of the group and to compare their identity with fellow students.

Activity 2 – My Dream

In this activity the students are asked to identify where they would like to be in five years' time, i.e. what they would like to be doing, thinking and feeling. They are asked to record these ideas around a self-portrait. Alternatively, it may be possible for the facilitator to arrange to have photos taken of each of the students. This would save time and also reduce any anxiety regarding the recording process.

Plenary

The facilitator may wish to focus on the following questions:

- ▸ What have we learnt about ourselves in this session?
- ▸ What have we learnt about each other in this session?
- ▸ How did we feel at the start of the session?
- ▸ How do we feel now at the end of the session?

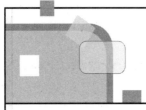

Identity

Record all the words that you can think of below.

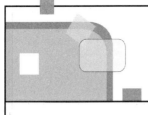

Identity

Facilitator's Notes

Thoughts	**Culture**
Belief	**Religion**
Feeling	**Principles**
Values	**Goals**
Politics	**Appearance**
Family	**Self-esteem**
Friends	**Confidence**
Likes/Dislikes	**Self-awareness**

Quick Activity

Pair up with another person.
You have 2 minutes to agree on the 3 biggest influences
on your IDENTITY. Use the brainstorm answers.
Be prepared to explain your choice!

3 Biggest Influences on My Identity
1.
2.
3.

Boys' World Group Rules

We all agree to keep the following rules
in our Boys' Group:

- _____

- _____

- _____

- _____

- _____

- _____

Signed: _____   **Date:** _____

Identity

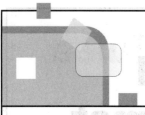

Joel is 13 years old and his mum's side of the family is from Jamaica and his dad's family is White British. Joel has always had a hard time fitting in with the 'white' kids at school and it has been hard proving himself to the 'black' kids. Joel really wants to be accepted by the 'black' crowd because he loves to rap but he also has some white friends that are not into that sort of thing. Joel's dad doesn't like him going round with 'the black crowd'. He says that they are all criminals and that they don't know how to wear their trousers properly. Joel doesn't know what to do because he just wants to be accepted but he doesn't know where he fits in.

Notes

Solution-focused problem-solving format

How does Joel feel?

What is the problem?

How would **Joel** feel and behave if this problem disappeared?

How would **Joel** know that he would no longer have this problem? What would be different?

What 3 things can **Joel** do now in order to remove this problem from his life?

1)

2)

3)

This is Me

My Music	My Hobbies	My Religion
My Appearance	**WHO AM I?**	My Politics
My Family	My Friends	My Likes/ Dislikes

Are you similar or different? Compare your identity with your fellow pupils.

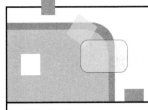

My Dream

Everyone has dreams. What are your dreams? Where would you like to be in 5 years' time? What do you want to be doing, thinking and feeling?

STOP, THINK and REFLECT.

Then complete the worksheet.

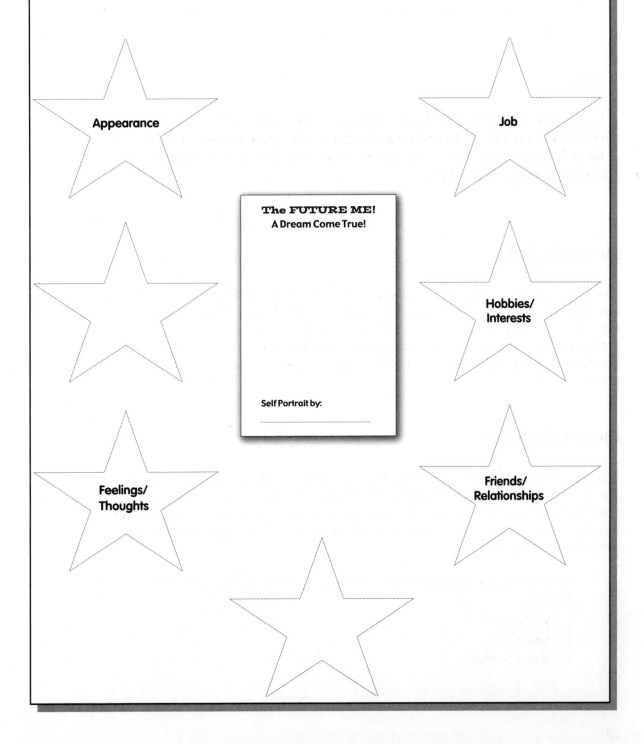

Appearance

Job

The FUTURE ME!
A Dream Come True!

Hobbies/
Interests

Self Portrait by:

Feelings/
Thoughts

Friends/
Relationships

Introduction

Students are asked to focus on the following question:

> What are some key words that you would use to describe the way someone looks?

Students can record their views on the blank Key Words Brainstorm sheet provided, or the facilitator may wish to record students' views on a whiteboard or flip-chart.

Tip

Model this for the students first and try to avoid negative words or phrases which can be picked up by students and used inappropriately. Keep it simple, e.g. Tall, short, black, white, etc. (see the Facilitator's Notes for some suggestions).

Brainstorm

Students are asked to brainstorm and to identify all the words and phrases that they can relate to this topic. The Facilitator can once again provide initial prompts if necessary. Students can record their ideas on the blank Key Words Brainstorm sheet provided, or the facilitator may wish to act as a scribe. This takes any stress out of the recording aspect and also tends to limit the more outrageous or negative words and phrases.

Quick Activity

Students are asked to work in pairs. The facilitator describes the task and explains to the students that this is a timed activity. They have two minutes to identify the three celebrities who have the most influence over the way young people dress. Ideas can be recorded on the Quick Activity sheet provided. It may be helpful to provide students with the following example:

> Three Celebrities who have the most influence over the way young people dress are:
>
> 1. 50 Cent.
> 2. Eminem.
> 3. David Beckham.

Circle Talk

The group rules can once again be reinforced prior to engaging in the circle talk activity. This activity utilises the Circle Time approach and students can be asked to focus upon the following questions:

▸ Is how we look important?

▸ Are people penalised for not conforming to stereotypes?

▸ What are the stereotypes we are presented with most frequently in the media?

▸ Is there such a thing as an ideal-looking person?

▸ Should only outside appearance matter or do we need to look inside as well?

Problem Scenario

The students are presented with the problem scenario entitled 'Appearance'. In this scenario, Nathan is wrongly accused of stealing from the local shops. He feels that this has happened because of the way he dresses, i.e. in baggy trousers and 'hoodies'. He feels that he has been labelled as a criminal because of this fact and doesn't think that he should change simply to avoid such stereotyping. Unfortunately his parents disagree and wish he would change his appearance to avoid these kinds of situations.

The facilitator can read the problem scenario to the students. Alternatively, students may wish to read the text by themselves or nominate another student to read it aloud. They can then make use of the Solution-focused Problem-solving Format in order to identify a way forward for Nathan. This involves identifying how Nathan feels, clarifying the problem and how Nathan might behave if the problem were removed, i.e. the miracle question idea. They are finally asked to identify three things that Nathan could do now in order to remove the problem from his life.

Activity Sheets

Activity 1 – Cool Dude Quiz

In this activity the students are asked to work with a partner and discuss a series of questions which relate to the quote at the top of the sheet: 'What you wear is who you are!'

Students are asked to discuss with a partner whether or not they agree with this statement and also to identify the kinds of clothes they like to wear and those they wouldn't like to wear. They are also asked to consider how they might feel if they couldn't afford fashionable clothes, i.e. to put themselves in the position of others who may be in such a situation.

Activity 2 – Look at Me! Working towards an Ideal Self

In this activity the students are asked to draw or photograph and label their particular features and then to draw and label themselves as they would want to look. They are then asked to consider how they can get nearer to their ideal appearance, i.e. what they would need to do in order to get there. They are asked to formulate specific targets and discuss these with a partner while also identifying who else can help them and how this may be done.

It is important here to emphasise the fact that an ideal self may be something that is entirely person specific. For example, one student may not be particularly concerned about being slightly overweight, whereas another might feel that this is something he wants to change. Another student may wish to have access to more fashionable clothes but not have the money to purchase them. Clearly, all these issues need to be handled with great sensitivity via the facilitator.

> **Tip**
>
> **Don't push for students to feed back here if there is the slightest hint of embarrassment. Be aware of boys whose self-esteem is very low and who feel unable to identify things about themselves that they might wish to change. If the activity is too challenging, then simply change the second part and ask students to identify their 'ideal person', i.e. someone they would aspire to be like in the future.**

Plenary

The facilitator may wish to focus on the following questions.

- ▸ Why is how we look important within our culture?
- ▸ Is this wrong or right?
- ▸ How did we feel about our appearance at the start of the session?

- How do we feel now about our appearance at the end of the session?

- Will having covered this topic make any difference in the way in which we look at other people and how they present themselves?

Tip

If the latter questions pose too much of a challenge to students, then simply focus on the first two.

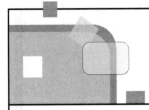

Appearance

Record all the words that you can think of below.

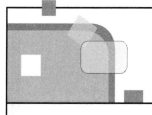

Appearance

Facilitator's Notes

Cool	Fat
Hip hop	Safe
Ugly	Bad
Good	Grunge
Hip	Skinny
Vile	Gangster
Labels	Brand names

Quick Activity

Pair up with another person.
You have 2 minutes to agree on and name the 3 celebrities
who have the most influence over the way young
people dress. Be prepared to explain your choice!

3 Celebrities who have the most influence over the way young people dress
1.
2.
3.

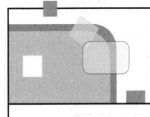

Appearance

Nathan wears baggy trousers and hoodies. When Nathan and his friends go into shops they are either watched closely by the shopkeepers or are accused of stealing. Nathan's parents think it is because of what they are wearing but Nathan doesn't think he should change what he is wearing to avoid these kinds of situations.

Notes

Solution-focused problem-solving format

How does **Nathan** feel?

What is the problem?

How would **Nathan** feel and behave if this problem disappeared?

How would **Nathan** know that he would no longer have this problem? What would be different?

What 3 things can **Nathan** do now in order to remove this problem from his life?

1)

2)

3)

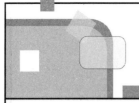

Cool Dude Quiz

'What you wear is who you are!'

Work with a partner and discuss the following questions:

Draw or find from a magazine a picture of a really cool-looking teenage boy:

Do you agree with the quote above?

☐ Yes

☐ No

If so, why? Tell your partner.

If not, why not? Tell your partner.

What clothes do you *like* to wear?

What clothes wouldn't you wear and why?

How would you feel if you couldn't afford cool clothes?

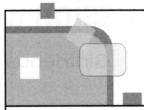

Look at me!

Working towards an Ideal Self

What I look like now:	**What I want to look like:**
Draw/Photograph and label.	Draw/Photograph and label.

How can you get nearer to your 'ideal' appearance? what do you need to do?

Record your targets and discuss with a partner.

1.

2.

3.

Who else can help you and how?

Introduction

Students are asked to focus on the following question:

> What words would you use to describe a girl?

Students can record their views on the blank Key Words Brainstorm sheet provided, or the facilitator may wish to record students' views on a whiteboard or flip-chart.

> **Tip**
>
> **The facilitator can model initial responses in order to steer the students away from making negative comments due to embarrassment or feelings of self-consciousness (see the Facilitator's Notes for some suggestions).**

Brainstorm

Students are asked to brainstorm and to identify all the words and phrases that they can relate to this topic. The facilitator can once again model initial responses in order to prompt thinking. Ideas can be recorded on the blank Key Words Brainstorm sheet provided, or the facilitator may wish to scribe the students' suggestions on a whiteboard or flip-chart.

Quick Activity

Students are asked to work in pairs. The facilitator describes the task and explains to the students that this is a timed activity. They have two minutes to identify the three most important qualities in a girl that is a friend. Ideas can be recorded on the Quick Activity sheet provided. It may be helpful to provide the students with the following example:

Three most important qualities in a girl that is a friend are:

1. You can talk to her and trust her, as she can keep a secret.
2. She will listen and won't laugh at you when you talk about your feelings, but she can also have a laugh.
3. She knows how other girls feel and behave so she'll be able to give you proper advice on relationships with girls and women.

Tip

Ensure that pairs are organised so that one student in each group can record responses with ease and also take a lead in terms of providing prompts and responses.

Circle Talk

The group rules can once again be reinforced prior to engaging in the circle talk activity. This activity utilises the Circle Time approach and students can be asked to focus upon the following questions:

▸ What is a girlfriend?

▸ What is a boyfriend?

▸ What are the differences between these relationships?

▸ Does a girlfriend have to be someone with whom you have a sexual or physical relationship?

▸ Can a girlfriend be the same kind of friend as a boy?

▸ What is the best thing a friend has ever done for us?

▸ What is the best thing that we have ever done for a friend?

▸ What is the worst thing a friend has ever done to us?

▸ What is the best thing that we have ever done to a friend?

Tip

The facilitator can provide answers to each question in order to act as a prompt and to model responses. This will also help to pre-empt any negative attention-seeking responses, e.g. 'A girl friend is someone you shag.' These should be noted and included in the discussion but not given undue attention. The response is clearly still valid, even if it may cause some embarrassed laughter from the group. It is most helpful for the facilitator to simply reframe the response, e.g. 'A girl friend is someone you may have sex with,' make a note and move on. The facilitator's script may be as follows: 'OK – yes, a girlfriend is someone that you might sleep with. I've got that. Now, what other definition can you offer me?'

Problem Scenario

The students are presented with the problem scenario entitled 'Girlfriends'. In this scenario, Frankie is becoming rather confused regarding his relationships. He has a girlfriend with whom he gets on well. However, she is not regarded as the best-looking girl in the school, unlike Brenda who has started to flirt openly with Frankie. His friends have begun to tease him about this situation and continually ask him why he doesn't choose the more attractive girl and get rid of his girlfriend.

The facilitator can read the problem scenario to the students. Alternatively, students may wish to read the text by themselves or nominate another student to read it aloud. They can then make use of the Solution-focused Problem-solving Format in order to identify a way forward for Frankie. This involves identifying how Frankie feels, clarifying the problem and how Frankie might behave if the problem were removed, i.e. the miracle question idea. They are finally asked to identify three things that Frankie could do now in order to remove the problem from his life.

Activity Sheets

Activity 1 – Girl Friend or *Girlfriend*?

In this activity the students are asked to describe a girlfriend and then to describe a girl who is a 'mate'. They are asked to consider whether a girl can be both at the same time and if so, why. If not, why not? The students are asked to discuss their ideas with a partner and then feed back to the whole group.

Activity 2 – Good Girls and Good Guys

In this activity the students are asked to consider the distinctions and differences between good and bad girl and boy friends. They are also asked to identify the similarities and finally to discuss who would be the best kind of girlfriend in the world and why?

Plenary

The facilitator may wish to focus on the following questions:

▸ What have we learnt about the nature of friendship?

▸ What would we consider to be a good girlfriend?

▸ What would we consider to be a good boyfriend?

▸ How can we be better friends to both our male friends and our female friends?

▸ How did we feel at the start of this session?

▸ How do we feel now at the end of the session?

Tip

If students don't appear to be able to cope with all the questions, then simply focus on the last three.

Developing Emotional Literacy with Teenage Boys

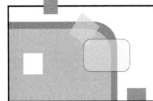

Key Words Brainstorm

Girls

Record all the words that you can think of below.

Girls

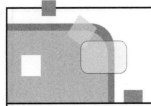

Facilitator's Notes

Friends	Fat/Phat
Slag	Warm
Sex	Safe
Gorgeous	Hot
Fit	Bird
Shag	

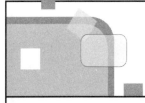

Quick Activity

Pair up with another person.
You have 2 minutes to agree on the 3 most important
qualities in a girl that is a friend.
Be prepared to explain your choice!

3 Most important qualities in a girl who is a friend

1.

2.

3.

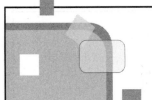

Girlfriends

Frankie has started seeing a girl named Cherie. He thinks she is pretty cool because she likes to just hang out and they like to do the same things. Only problem is that Cherie isn't the best-looking girl at school and the guys are all after Brenda who is really fit. Brenda has been flirting with Frankie in front of the boys and it is pretty obvious that Brenda is interested in Frankie. The boys have started to tease Frankie about Cherie and say things like, 'Why are you with that when you could have Brenda?'

Notes

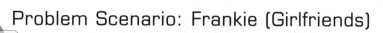

Problem Scenario: Frankie (Girlfriends)

Solution-focused problem-solving format

How does **Frankie** feel?

What is the problem?

How would **Frankie** feel and behave if this problem disappeared?

How would **Frankie** know that he would no longer have this problem? What would be different?

What 3 things can **Frankie** do now in order to remove this problem from his life?

1)

2)

3)

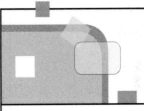

Girl friend or Girlfriend?

When is a girl your friend who you love and when is she just another mate? What is the difference? Record your ideas in the chart below.

Words to describe a GIRLFRIEND	Words to describe a GIRL who is your MATE

Can a girl be both at the same time? If so, why? If not, why not?

Discuss your ideas with a partner and then feed back to the whole group. One of you can feed back. We can then compare similarities and differences between our ideas.

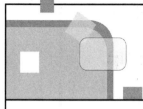

Good Girls and Good Guys

GOOD girl/boy friends What are their qualities?	**BAD** girl/boy friends What are their qualities?
☐ Good listener	☐ Doesn't listen
☐	☐
☐	☐
☐	☐

What are the differences/similarities?

Differences	Similarities

Brainstorm

Work with a friend and record your ideas in response to the following question:

Who would be the best girlfriend in the world and why?

Introduction

Students are asked to focus on the following question:

What words come to your mind when you think of friendship?

Students can record their views on the blank Key Words Brainstorm sheet provided, or the facilitator may wish to record students' views on a whiteboard or flip-chart.

Tip

The facilitator can model initial thoughts and responses here in order to prompt the students (see the Facilitator's Notes for some suggestions). It may also be helpful to make a thesaurus available for some students.

Brainstorm

Students are asked to brainstorm and to identify all the words and phrases that they can relate to this topic. The facilitator may choose to model initial responses again. Ideas can be recorded on the blank Key Words Brainstorm sheet provided, or the facilitator may wish to scribe the students' suggestions on a whiteboard or flip-chart.

Quick Activity

Students are asked to work in pairs. The facilitator describes the task and explains to the students that this is a timed activity. They have two minutes to identify the three most important qualities that they think make a good mate. Ideas can be recorded on the Quick Activity sheet provided. It may be helpful to provide students with the following example:

Three most important qualities that make a good mate are:

1. You can have a laugh with them.
2. They can be trusted to keep things secret.
3. They are there for you.

Circle Talk

The group rules can once again be reinforced prior to engaging in the circle talk activity. This activity utilises the Circle Time approach and students can be asked to focus upon the following questions:

- What kind of pressures do boys experience?

- What pressures do boys put on other boys?

- Is there a pressure to be part of the crew in school?

- What happens to people who are not included in crews?

- Do you think people can really benefit from being in a crew? If so, how?

- Have you ever felt left out of a group?

- How did you cope with this?

- Have you ever left anyone else out of a group?

- How do you think he/she coped with it?

Problem Scenario

The students are presented with the problem scenario entitled 'Friendships'. In this scenario, Lee is becoming increasingly tense and worried because of the way in which his friends have been behaving. They frequently verbally abuse people they meet on the street and regard this as good entertainment. However, they have recently become aware of the happy-slapping culture and are consequently planning to target their first victim in the near future.

The facilitator can read the problem scenario to the students. Alternatively, students may wish to read the text by themselves or nominate another student to read it aloud. They can then make use of the Solution-focused Problem-solving Format in order to identify a way forward for Lee. This involves identifying how Lee feels, clarifying the problem and how Lee might behave if the problem were removed, i.e. the miracle question idea. They are finally asked to identify three things that Lee could do now in order to remove the problem from his life.

Activity Sheets

Activity 1 – The Crew Quiz

In this activity the students are asked to work with a partner and take it in turns to interview each other using the list of questions provided. This reinforces the content covered in the circle talk phase of the session, which allows students to focus in more detail on their own personal experiences within a more private context, i.e. this is a paired activity.

Tip

It may be helpful to video these interviews for future reference. We have found this strategy extremely useful when dealing with the most disaffected group of boys. The thought of being immortalised on camera can have a calming effect (once the initial excitement has died down) and really helps to focus the students. Naturally, permission needs to have been gained from parents/carers and the students themselves.

Activity 2 – Investigation Internet!

In this activity the students are asked to find out some facts about crews by accessing the internet. They are asked to find out about a fight or confrontation that took place between two crews and to identify triggers and outcomes. Once all the information has been collected they are then asked to present it as a speech or talk. The facilitator may wish to video these presentations in order to screen them for the rest of the group and invite comments and prompt further discussion.

Plenary

The facilitator may wish to focus on the following questions:

▸ What have we learnt about our ability to cope with peer pressure in this session?

▸ What have we learnt about the impact of crews and gangs in this session?

▸ How do we feel about this topic now?

▸ Is this different to how we felt about it at the start of the session?

▸ What advice would we give to someone who was feeling pressured to participate in a crew?

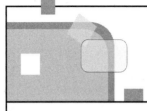

Friendship

Record all the words that you can
think of below.

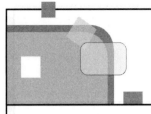

Friendship

Facilitator's Notes

Trust	Gang
Truth	Pressure
Mate	Kind
Watch out	Support
Loyal	Crew

Quick Activity

Pair up with another person.
You have 2 minutes to agree on the 3 most important
qualities that you think make a good mate.
Be prepared to explain your choice!

3 most important qualities that you think make a good mate

1.

2.

3.

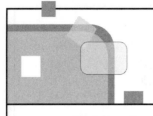

Friendships

Lee goes out with his mates every day. They usually end up on the high street looking for trouble. Lee and his mates love a good laugh and are usually having one at someone else's expense. Most of the time they call people on the street names but sometimes they take things too far. Lee likes his friends but sometimes he feels uncomfortable about what they get involved in. Lately, they have been planning to 'happy slap' someone; they pick a random person to slap and record it on their phone to show to others. Lee really doesn't want to be involved in this but is worried that his friends will 'take the mick out of him' if he says anything. Lee knows it's going to happen soon but he doesn't know what he should do about it.

Notes

Problem Scenario: Lee (Friendships)

Solution-focused problem-solving format

How does **Lee** feel?

What is the problem?

How would **Lee** feel and behave if this problem disappeared?

How would **Lee** know that he would no longer have this problem? What would be different?

What 3 things can **Lee** do now in order to remove this problem from his life?

1)

2)

3)

The Crew Quiz

Work with a partner. Take it in turns to interview each other using the following list of questions:

1. What is a crew? How do you define it?

2. Have you ever been a member of a crew?

3. How did you feel? What positive differences did you see?

4. What negative things did you feel or do?

5. Is there pressure to be part of a crew?

6. If you were going to start a crew, how would you do it?

7. What happens to people who are not included?

8. Do you think people 'grow out' of being in a crew? If so, why?

9. What kinds of things do older people do that may be similar?

Investigation Internet!

Find out some FACTS about CREWS.

Work with a partner and use the internet to access the following information:

☐ Find out about a fight or confrontation that took place between two crews.

☐ What triggered it off?

☐ What was the outcome?

☐ Was it positive or negative?

☐ What do you think about the situation? Who was 'right' and who was 'wrong' and why?

☐ How would you have felt if you had been involved in the situation?

☐ What do you think could have been done in order to prevent the confrontation in the first place?

Collect all the information and then present it as a speech/talk. Ask the course facilitator to video your presentation (which should last approximately 5 minutes). It can then be screened for the rest of the group.

Introduction

Students are asked to focus on the following question:

What words do you think of when you hear the word sex?

Students can record their views on the blank Key Words Brainstorm sheet provided, or the facilitator may wish to record students' views on a whiteboard or flip-chart.

Tip

It is vital from the outset that the facilitator is confident and unembarrassed by the content and subject matter of this session. No sense of embarrassment should be transferred to the students. The whole topic needs to be dealt with in a matter of fact and down to earth manner. Responses to the introduction, brainstorm and circle talk phases of the session all need to be appropriately modelled by the facilitator (see the Facilitator's Notes for some suggestions).

Brainstorm

Students are asked to brainstorm and to identify all the words and phrases that they can relate to this topic. Ideas can be recorded on the blank Key Words Brainstorm sheet provided, or the facilitator may wish to scribe the students' suggestions on a whiteboard or flip-chart.

Quick Activity

Students are asked to work in pairs. The facilitator describes the task and explains to the students that this is a timed activity. They have two minutes to identify the three most popular reasons for not having sex. Ideas can be recorded on the Quick Activity sheet provided. It may be helpful to provide students with the following example:

Three most popular reasons for not having sex are:

1. Getting AIDS.
2. Not having protection.
3. Saving it for the right person.

Circle Talk

The group rules can once again be reinforced prior to engaging in the circle talk activity. This activity utilises the Circle Time approach and students can be asked to focus upon the following questions:

▸ How do we currently feel about sex?

▸ What words come to mind when we hear this term?

▸ Is it possible for young people to have safe sex and feel positive about their bodies and sexual activities?

▸ How do adults perceive young peoples' sex lives?

▸ Are these perceptions negative or positive?

▸ How do we define safe sex?

Problem Scenarios

The students are presented with the problem scenario entitled 'Sex'. In this scenario, Saeed is concerned about his lack of experience with girls. He is very shy and worried that he may be made to feel a fool if his friends find out that he has never kissed a girl, let alone had sex. He does, however, meet a girl in the local park and spends an hour on his own with her, chatting and generally getting to know her. Later, when quizzed by his friends, he lies and provides them with a graphic description of this supposed intimate encounter.

The facilitator can read the problem scenario to the students. Alternatively, students may wish to read the text to themselves or nominate another student to read it aloud. They can then make use of the Solution-focused Problem-solving Format in order to identify a way forward for Saeed. This involves identifying how Saeed feels, clarifying the problem and how Saeed might behave if the problem were removed, i.e. the miracle question idea. They are finally asked to identify three things that Saeed could do now in order to remove the problem from his life.

Activity Sheets

Activity 1 – Sex Quiz

In this activity the students are asked to identify whether each of the statements is true or false. Statements include definitions of sex such as 'Sex is a laugh/dirty/only for people who are married/best if you love the other person,' etc. The idea here is to dispel any myths. The facilitator has the opportunity to feed back the most accurate responses once the students have completed the quiz.

Activity 2 – HIV/AIDS Quiz: Fact and Fiction

Once again in this activity the students are presented with a range of statements. They are asked to tick those they identify as facts and put a cross beside those they consider to be fictions. Once again the idea is to promote accurate information and dispel any myths, prejudices or stereotypes held by the boys within the group. Answers have been provided on a separate sheet.

Tip

Be aware that some young men will express homophobic views. This is very often an aspect of adolescent development. Students should not be reprimanded but praised for being open and honest and then immediately challenged to justify their views. It may also be helpful for the facilitator to complete the quiz alongside the students so as to model responses as part of the feedback.

Plenary

The facilitator may wish to focus on the following questions:

▶ What have we learnt about our attitudes towards sex in this session?

▶ Have we increased our knowledge of HIV/AIDS?

▶ How did we feel about this talk at the start of the session?

▶ How do we feel about it at the end of the session?

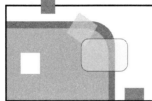

Key Words Brainstorm

Sex

Record all the words that you can
think of below.

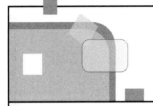

Sex

Facilitator's Notes

Pornography	**Prostitutes**
STIs	**Partner**
Durex	**Power**
Pleasure	**AIDS**
Pregnancy	**Contraception**
Rape	**Love**
Harassment	**Virginity**
Ejaculation	**Abortion**

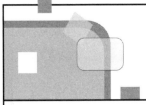

Quick Activity

Pair up with another person.
You have 2 minutes to agree on the 3 most common
reasons for not having sex.
Be prepared to explain your choice!

3 Most popular reasons for not having sex
1.
2.
3.

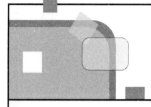

Sex

Saeed is 13 years old and has never kissed a girl but all of his mates think he has. Saeed has always been interested in girls but he is shy and doesn't want to be made a fool of. One evening he meets a girl at the park through his group of friends. They decide to go off to a more secluded part of the park to get away from the crowd. They chat for an hour and then she tells Saeed she needs to go home. The next day at school David asks Saeed with a cheeky grin, 'So how was it in the bushes with Sara last night?' Saeed eagerly retells a graphic story about their intimate encounter, none of which is true of course.

Notes

Solution-focused problem-solving format

How does **Saeed** feel?

What is the problem?

How would **Saeed** feel and behave if this problem disappeared?

How would **Saeed** know that he would no longer have this problem? What would be different?

What 3 things can **Saeed** do now in order remove this problem from his life?

1)

2)

3)

Sex Quiz

Stop! Think! Reflect!

What do you think? Tick either true or false.

	T	F
Sex is … A laugh Dirty Only for people who are married Best if you love the other person The same as intercourse Something you don't talk about in public A good way to sell magazines		
Women don't need/want as much sex as men		
A man always wants sex		
A man can't be good at sex unless he's got a big penis		
A man's orgasm is the same as a woman's		
Women can suffer from premature ejaculation (coming too soon)		
Only men and boys can masturbate		
A man should take the lead when having sex		
A woman can't be good at sex unless she's got big breasts		
Gay men and lesbians enjoy sex in just the same way as straight men and women		

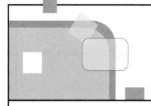

HIV/AIDS Quiz

Fact and Fiction

Put a tick beside those statements you consider to be FACTS and a cross beside those you consider to be FICTION.

1. You can get the HIV virus from:

- A toilet seat
- Sharing needles
- Masturbation
- Mosquitoes biting you
- Getting a tattoo
- Having your nose/belly button pierced
- Using drugs of any kind

- Sharing a glass or a canned drink with a friend
- Giving First Aid to someone
- Swimming in a public pool or in the sea
- Having sex with lots of different people
- Having sex with a person who is HIV positive
- Kissing someone
- Sharing razors with someone

- Going to the dentist for a checkup
- Using someone else's toothbrush
- Getting a love bite from someone
- Mouth-to-mouth resuscitation
- Having a blood transfusion in hospital
- Giving blood

2. The following groups have more of a chance of catching the virus:

- Gay boys/men
- Prostitutes
- Heterosexual men and women
- People who are haemophiliacs
- Lesbians

- Young people/children
- Drug addicts/users
- African people
- Bisexuals
- None of these

3. The HIV virus and AIDS originally came from:

- Japan
- New York
- The CIA
- The KGB

- Africa
- Green monkeys
- Outer space
- None of these

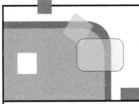

HIV/AIDS Quiz

4. You can get an HIV test:

From your doctor

From Boots/Superdrug

At a family planning clinic

From an STI (VD) clinic

5. If someone has the HIV virus:

They should not give blood

They will die eventually

They should not have babies at all

They should not have sex at all

They are infectious to everyone else

6. The following symptoms show that a person has AIDS:

Constant tiredness

Weight loss

Swollen glands

Diarrhoea

Fever, chills and night sweats

Purple blotches on their skin

White spots in their mouths

A dry cough

None of these

All of these

7. If someone has AIDS:

They should not have sex with anyone

They should not be isolated

They are going to die

They should stop work at once

All of these

None of these

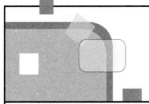

HIV/AIDS Quiz

8. Who should you tell if you have the HIV virus:

- Your GP
- Your boyfriend/girlfriend

- Your life insurance company
- Anyone else you choose

9. If a friend has the virus, you should:

- Tell their family
- Give them all the support you can

- Avoid touching them or going near them
- Stop seeing them altogether

10. Which of the following ways of having sex are safe?

- Oral sex
- Anal sex without a condom
- Heavy petting

- Masturbation
- Kissing
- Vaginal intercourse

HIV/AIDS Quiz

Facts and Fiction

Answer sheet

1. The **Human Immunodeficiency Virus (HIV) is transmitted through the passing of certain bodily fluids (semen, vaginal and cervical secretions, blood, blood products, and organ transplants) from one person to another**. Evidence suggests that kissing, love bites, using public toilets, mosquito bites, swimming in a public pool, using someone's toothbrush, sharing a glass, and masturbation are all safe activities. As long as equipment has been sterilised properly, tattooing, going to the dentist and ear piercing are also safe activities. Furthermore, giving blood is safe because clean equipment is used every time. Reasonable precautions should be taken when performing First Aid and mouth-to-mouth resuscitation. It is strongly advised to not share sex toys and razors as these can carry bodily fluids. As information changes all the time it is advisable to keep up to date with information from services such as the Terence Higgins Trust and the National Aidsline.

2. It is not who people are but what they do that puts them at risk. **Therefore none of these groups have more of a chance of contracting HIV**.

3. **We do not know where HIV/AIDS originated**. However, this is often a delicate question as it is used to stir up racial tension. For example, Africa has been blamed for its origin.

4. **To get an HIV test you can visit an STI (VD) clinic**. However, it is important to take an additional test 3 to 4 months after a possible exposure as it often takes this long to incubate.

5. **People with the HIV virus are infectious and therefore need to take precautions so that they do not pass the virus on**. Giving blood is not an option. Pregnancy is still an option but can put a strain on the immune system, which is something to be considered. Furthermore, babies born from HIV positive mothers are not automatically born HIV positive.

6. **All of these could be symptoms of AIDS but they could also be symptoms of another viral infection**. If someone is concerned, the best thing to do is to get themselves checked.

7. **None of these**. People with AIDS can have safe sex, they should not be isolated and many work until they feel they are too ill. Most people with AIDS will die of the syndrome but with new treatments and more scientific knowledge, more people are living longer.

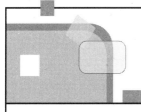

HIV/AIDS Quiz

8. **If you have AIDS, it is up to you who you tell**. It is important to have someone whom you can receive support from. Also it might be important in certain situations to inform people if you feel that your actions have or could have put them at risk. It is also important to consider that some people might discriminate against you. People have been fired for being HIV positive and some life insurance policies might not cover you if you have taken a test.

9. **If you have a friend who has the virus, it is important to give them all the support you can.** This can include hugging and cuddling. It is important to also respect their wishes as to whether they choose to tell anyone else or not.

10. Heavy petting, kissing and masturbation are low-risk activities. **Anal sex and vaginal sex without a condom are high-risk activities. Oral sex without a condom is a medium-risk activity.**

Session 6

Problem Solving

Introduction

Students are asked to focus on the following questions:

> How do we currently solve problems?
> What skills do we use?

Students can record their views on the blank Key Words Brainstorm sheet provided, or the facilitator may wish to record students' views on a whiteboard or flip-chart.

Tip

The facilitator can initially model responses in order to prompt students' thinking (see the Facilitator's Notes for some suggestions).

Brainstorm

Students are asked to brainstorm and to identify all the words and phrases that they can relate to this topic. Ideas can be recorded on the blank Key Words Brainstorm sheet provided, or the facilitator may wish to scribe the students' suggestions on a whiteboard or flip-chart.

Tip

The facilitator may wish to prompt thinking by actually explaining the win–win, win–lose, lose–lose distinctions. This may be a relatively new concept for some of the students and they may require such additional explanation at the outset. This does pre-empt the first activity to some extent, but as the vocabulary may be new to many in the group, we would suggest that it is helpful to introduce these concepts/distinctions at this point in the session.

Quick Activity

Students are asked to work in pairs. The facilitator describes the task and explains to the students that this is a timed activity. They have two minutes to identify three reasons why all people should aim to improve their problem-solving skills. Ideas can be recorded on the Quick Activity sheet provided. It may be helpful to provide students with the following example:

Three reasons why all people should aim to improve their problem-solving skills are:

1. It can reduce stress.
2. You can get along better with other people.
3. It makes life easier for you and everyone around you.

Circle Talk

The group rules can once again be reinforced prior to engaging in the circle talk activity. This activity utilises the Circle Time approach and students can be asked to focus upon the following questions:

▸ If we get angry about something, how do we react?

▸ How do we cope with problems?

▸ Who helps us to solve problems?

▸ How can we ensure that we get better at solving problems in the future?

Tip

Prompt the students to think about how their body, thoughts and feelings change when a problem arises and to specifically identify how they can tell when they are going to 'lose it'.

Problem Scenario

The students are presented with the problem scenario entitled 'Problem Solving'. In this scenario, Sean is finding it difficult to cope in Maths lessons. This is mainly due to the fact that he cannot understand the work he's asked to do. He is becoming increasingly angry and embarrassed because the other students in his group appear to be able to complete the work without difficulty. He starts to misbehave in the lessons and this leads to a verbal confrontation with the teacher. This pattern is beginning to become a regular occurrence and there seems to be no solution.

The facilitator can read the problem scenario to the students. Alternatively, students may wish to read the text to themselves or nominate another student to read it aloud. They can then make use of the Solution-focused Problem-solving Format in order to identify a way forward for Sean. This involves identifying how Sean feels, clarifying the problem and how Sean might behave if the problem were removed, i.e. the miracle question idea. They are finally asked to identify three things that Sean could do now in order to remove the problem from his life.

Activity Sheets

Activity 1 – Conflict Information

The first activity is intended to provide the students with information as to the possible results of conflict and a means of mediating specific difficulties that they may encounter within both the school and the social context. The Conflict Information sheet details three possible results of the conflict as follows:

- Win–win
- Win–lose
- Lose–lose

Activity 2 – Talk Time Activity

Within a brief talk time activity the students are asked to consider a time when they were in conflict with someone else and to try and identify the outcome and why it ended in that particular way. They are asked to describe the situation to a partner and then to feed it back to the rest of the group. Students can then be asked to identify similarities and differences in the situations that they have described.

Tip

To avoid further confrontations or conflicts, make a rule of not using names, i.e. not identifying who the conflict was with. Talking in the third person may also be helpful here.

Activity 3 – The Mediation Process

The Mediation Process sheet describes the five steps involved in mediation. Students are asked to get into teams of three, allocating roles as follows:

Student 1, Student 2 and Mediator

They are asked to choose a problem from the problem cards provided. This sheet can be photocopied onto card. The cards can then be cut up and given to students within the session. The students are asked to work through one of the problems, with each student in the group taking on the prescribed role. The facilitator can then video the mediations and they can be reviewed by the group as a whole and discussed as appropriate.

Plenary

The facilitator may wish to focus on the following questions:

- What have we learnt about the mediation process in this session?
- What have we learnt about our own problem-solving skills?

- Have we learnt how to further develop our problem-solving skills?

- How and when would we use these skills in the future?

- Can we think of examples at this point in time?

Tip

If the students can't think of an example, the facilitator can provide one that reinforces the importance of developing these skills. One example might be when we are in the work situation and someone takes credit for something we have done, or someone does not contribute as much to a piece of work and yet takes credit from the boss.

Problem Solving

Record all the words that you can think of below.

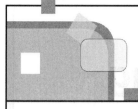

Problem Solving

Facilitator's Notes

Negotiate	**Win–win**
Agree	**Win–lose**
Disagree	**Lose–lose**
Turns	**Active listening**
Compromise	**Plan**
Assertive	

Quick Activity

Pair up with another person.
You have 2 minutes to agree on 3 reasons why all people
should aim to improve their problem-solving skills.
Be prepared to explain your choice!

3 Reasons why all people should aim to improve their problem-solving skills
1.
2.
3.

Problem Solving

Sean really struggles to understand his maths work. Every lesson, after the teacher explains and sets the work to be done, Sean looks around to see everyone scribbling away totally confident in what they are doing, while Sean still doesn't have a clue where to begin. So immediately he starts throwing scraps of crumbled pieces of paper at his mate on the other side of the room. The teacher warns him to stop but he doesn't because the whole class is laughing and encouraging him to continue. The teacher then blows, they verbally argue for ten minutes and then he is sent to the office. This is a typical Maths lesson for Sean.

Notes

Solution-focused problem-solving format

How does **Sean** feel?

What is the problem?

How would **Sean** feel and behave if this problem disappeared?

How would **Sean** know that he would no longer have this problem? What would be different?

What 3 things can **Sean** do now in order to remove this problem from his life?

1)

2)

3)

Conflict Information

There are 3 possible results of a conflict:

1. WIN–WIN

The problem is sorted out without aggression as:

(a) both people negotiate and cooperate

(b) they reach a compromise

(c) no one gets hurt

(d) both people respect themselves and each other

2. WIN–LOSE

The problem isn't sorted out because one person becomes aggressive and the other gives in so:

(a) one person gets hurt

(b) one person gets their own way

(c) both people do not show respect for each other or themselves

3. LOSE–LOSE

The problem isn't sorted out because both people are aggressive and:

(a) both people get hurt (emotionally and/or physically)

(b) things end up worse

(c) both people lose respect for themselves and each other

(d) no one is a winner!

Talk Time Activity

 Think of a time when you were in conflict with someone else.

Try to identify the outcome and why it ended up this way.

Describe your situation to a partner and then feed it back to the rest of the group.

Discuss any similarities and differences in the situations you have described.

The Mediation Process

Stop!
Think!
Reflect!
Act it out!

Get into teams of 3 and allocate roles:

Student 1, Student 2 and Mediator

Choose a problem from the cards provided and then work through the mediation process taking on your roles. The course facilitator can then video your mediation and this can be viewed by the group as a whole.

STEP 1
• The mediator introduces him/herself
• The mediator agrees not to take sides
• The mediator agrees not to offer any solutions
• The students agree to speak one at a time and not interrupt each other
• They agree to show respect and not to blame or accuse each other

STEP 2
• The mediator asks each student to describe the problem and how he feels
• The mediator then repeats back what has been said

STEP 3
• The mediator asks each student to describe how the other feels

STEP 4
• The mediator asks each pupil for suggestions

STEP 5
• The mediator then asks both students to a agree to a solution

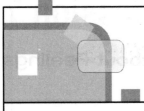

Problem Cards

1. **Ben and Max** are brothers and they are always fighting over time on the internet at home. Mum and Dad aren't always there to 'ref' so they end up fist fighting.

2. **Malik and Wesley** are best mates. Lately Kai is only interested in smoking weed and Malik isn't keen. Since Kai has been smoking they seem to fight all the time.

3. **Jamie** stole cash from his art teacher's purse. When the school accused him, he asked his friend **Matt** to take the blame. Jamie would be formerly charged as he already had a list of incidents and Matt has none. Matt doesn't want to take the blame.

4. **Paul and Chris** are always winding each other up at break times. They don't get on and are always name calling. As a result they are also always getting in trouble with the teachers; they get sent to the office and parents get called daily.

5. **Liam and Laura** always pick on each other in class but Liam is always the one that gets in trouble because he reacts the 'loudest'. The teachers are threatening to call in both sets of parents to try to resolve the issue.

6. **Mr Smith** is in charge of organising work experience and college for the pupils but he doesn't think Harvinder is ready or mature enough. Harvinder has argued with him but he says he has to prove it to him.

7. Think of your own.

8. Think of your own.

Introduction

Students are asked to focus on the following questions:

Do boys talk less about their feelings than girls?
If so, why do you think this is the case?

Students can record their views on the blank Key Words Brainstorm sheet provided, or the facilitator may wish to record students' views on a whiteboard or flip-chart.

Tip

The facilitator can provide initial prompts to start the students off (see the Facilitator's Notes for some suggestions).

Brainstorm

Students are asked to brainstorm and to identify all the words and phrases that they can relate to this topic. The facilitator can once again provide initial prompts if necessary. Students can record their ideas on the blank Key Words Brainstorm sheet provided, or the facilitator may wish to scribe the students' responses on a whiteboard or flip-chart.

Quick Activity

Students are asked to work in pairs. The facilitator describes the task and explains to the students that this is a timed activity. They have two minutes to identify the three feelings they like the most. Ideas can be recorded on the Quick Activity sheet provided. It may be helpful to provide students with the following example:

Three feelings I like the most are:

1. Happiness.
2. Love.
3. Excitement.

Circle Talk

The group rules can once again be reinforced prior to engaging in the circle talk activity. This activity utilises the Circle Time approach and students can be asked to focus upon the following questions:

- ▸ How many feelings can we name?

- ▸ What is our most comfortable feeling?

- ▸ What is our most uncomfortable feeling?

- ▸ How do we currently deal with uncomfortable feelings?

- ▸ What strategies do we have?

- ▸ Is it harder for boys to talk about feelings than girls?

- ▸ Why do we think this might be the case?

- ▸ Do we think boys should talk more about their feelings and express their ideas more openly?

- ▸ If so, why?

- ▸ If not, why not?

- ▸ What do we think happens to younger men who are unable to express their feelings?

- ▸ What impact could this have on their mental well-being in the future?

> **Tip**
>
> **Use an egg timer (1, 2 or 3 minutes) when focusing on the first question and act as a scribe for the group, e.g. 'How many feelings can we name around the circle in 2 minutes? Go!'**

Problem Scenario

The students are presented with the problem scenario entitled 'Talking about Feelings'. In this scenario Brett is concerned about his best friend John. John's mother has been recently killed in a terrible accident. Initially Brett feels he is able to support John but then begins to feel increasingly helpless as John becomes more depressed. John feels unable to communicate and begins to isolate himself. Brett consequently doesn't know how to help his friend and feels useless and powerless in this situation.

The facilitator can read the problem scenario to the students. Alternatively, students may wish to read the text to themselves or nominate another student to read it aloud. They can then make use of the Solution-focused Problem-solving Format in order to identify a way forward for Brett. This involves identifying how Brett feels, clarifying the problem and how Brett might behave if the problem were removed, i.e. the miracle question idea. They are finally asked to identify three things that Brett could currently do now in order to remove the problem from his life.

Activity Sheets

Activity 1 – Talking about Feelings

In this activity the students are asked to consider a series of 18 statements identifying how they would feel if their best friend moved away, they were mugged, they won the lottery, etc. The idea here is to elicit one-word responses as rapidly as possible. Clearly if some of the boys feel able to provide more in-depth answers, then this will be useful in terms of modelling emotional responses to others within the group.

Tip

It is important not to put any pressure on students to provide more detailed responses. This needs to be a voluntary process.

Activity 2 – Personal Profile

In this activity students are asked to work on their own and think about the times when they have experienced the following feelings:

Anger, fear, sadness, happiness, excitement, etc.

They are then asked to discuss these times with a partner using the script provided. The idea here is to provide the students with a framework for discussing feelings so that they feel safe and comfortable in doing this and do not feel to any extent exposed.

Plenary

The facilitator may wish to focus on the following questions:

▸ What have we learnt about our feelings in this session?

▸ What have we learnt about other people's feelings in this session?

▸ How did we feel when we began this session?

▸ How do we feel now at the end of this session?

Tip

By this point in the programme, we would hope that the majority of students should be able to offer a response to each question. All responses need to be validated and praised – even if they are short one-word answers. It is important not to forget, however, that this activity may still pose problems for some individuals.

Talking about Feelings

Record all the words that you can think of below.

Talking about Feelings

Facilitator's Notes

Empathy	Disclosure
Vocabulary	Acceptance of self
Only for girls	Not cool
Self-awareness	Confidence
Listening	Observing
Problem solving	Feeling
Mental health	Self-management
Self-esteem	'I' messages
Being vulnerable	

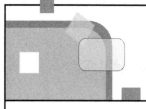

Quick Activity

Pair up with another person.
You have 2 minutes to agree on 3 feelings you like the most.
Be prepared to explain your choice!

3 Feelings I like the most
1.
2.
3.

Talking about Feelings

Brett has been best mates with John for as long as he can remember. What he likes most about John is that he always makes Brett laugh. John never feels sorry for himself and always takes Brett's mind off things when Brett is getting hassled by his parents. John is almost always happy and Brett likes that because his home life can be a bit depressing. One day there is a terrible accident and John's mum is killed. Brett does all the things a mate would do like go to the funeral, buy flowers, etc. However, the hard part comes weeks after when John doesn't seem to be

getting better. He is always depressed, doesn't want to come out and just watches TV all the time. Brett doesn't know what to do or what to say. John always made him smile and now he feels he can't return the favour.

Notes

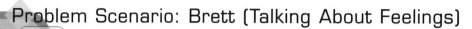

Problem Scenario: Brett (Talking About Feelings)

Solution-focused problem-solving format

How does **Brett** feel?

What is the problem?

How would **Brett** feel and behave if this problem disappeared?

How would **Brett** know that he would no longer have this problem? What would be different?

What 3 things can **Brett** do now in order to remove this problem from his life?

1)

2)

3)

Talking about Feelings

Talk in a circle. How would you feel if:

Your parent/carer told you that they were proud of you	You were mugged	Your parent/carer got cancer
You lost all your money	Your date got drunk at a party and went off with someone else	Your big brother beat you up
Your work was the best in the class	You didn't make the team	The girl you liked said yes when you asked her out
You couldn't understand the work	You ruined your designer trainers	Your friend was killed in a car crash
You were being bullied	You had an accident and lost the use of your legs	You won the lottery
Your clothes were rubbish	Someone stole your mobile	Your best friend moved away

Name the feeling and say why you would feel like this.

Personal Profile

Work on your own and think about the times you experienced the following feelings:

Anger	Appreciated	Sadness	Happiness	Excitement
Lovely	Liked	Jealous	Tension	Upset
Panic	Annoyed	Irritated	Confident	Peaceful
Loved	Grateful	Fear	Moody	Hurt

Discuss these times with a partner using the following script:

(a) I felt _____ when _____.

(b) When I felt _____ I did _____.

(c) I thought _____.

(d) On reflection, I could have _____.

(e) If I feel like this again, I will _____.

Introduction

Students are asked to focus on the following questions:

> What legal drugs can we name and what illegal drugs can we name?
> Why is this distinction made?

Students can record their views on the blank Key Words Brainstorm sheet provided, or the facilitator may wish to record students' views on a whiteboard or flip-chart.

Tip

After providing initial prompts if necessary (see the Facilitator's Notes for some suggestions), the facilitator can read students' ideas and explore them in a non-judgemental way. Students need to feel able to be open and honest without fear of judgement. Also, it is important to be very matter of fact in your approach here so as not to sensationalise the issues.

Brainstorm

Students are asked to brainstorm and to identify all the words and phrases that they can relate to this topic. The facilitator may choose to model initial responses again. Ideas can be recorded on the blank Key Words Brainstorm sheet, or the facilitator may wish to scribe the students' suggestions on a whiteboard or flip-chart.

Quick Activity

Students are asked to work in pairs. The facilitator describes the task and explains to the students that this is a timed activity. They have two minutes to identify the three most popular reasons for taking drugs. Ideas can be recorded on the Quick Activity sheet provided. It may be helpful to provide students with the following example:

Three most popular reasons for taking drugs are:

1. To be hard.
2. Others trying it.
3. The buzz.

Circle Talk

The group rules can once again be reinforced prior to engaging in the circle talk activity. This activity utilises the Circle Time approach and students can be asked to focus upon the following questions:

- How much do we know about drugs?
- How much do we know about legal drugs and illegal drugs?
- What effects do some drugs have on us?
- Is this healthy or unhealthy?
- How can we maintain our own emotional and physical well-being if we participate in taking drugs?

> ## Tip
>
> **The facilitator can give the first response to the initial question, e.g. I know that we use certain drugs to relieve pain or cure illnesses such as cancer. This will help to normalise the topic and steer students away from making more sensationalised contributions. However, as usual, the facilitator needs to listen to and include all views but simply move on quickly to the next point or contribution if it becomes clear that someone is showing off or becoming self-conscious.**

Problem Scenario

The students are presented with the problem scenario entitled 'Drugs Awareness'. In this scenario, George is feeling pressurised and worried because his two best friends are becoming increasingly obsessed with smoking illegal substances. George is concerned for them because they are both becoming more moody and forgetful. George also feels pressured to join in and doesn't want to lose his friends by not conforming to their expectations. He is also worried about their health and the fact that they are not good to be around when they are stoned.

The facilitator can read the problem scenario to the students. Alternatively, students may wish to read the text to themselves or nominate another student to read it aloud. They can then make use of the Solution-focused Problem-solving Format in order to identify a way forward for George. This involves identifying how George feels, clarifying the problem and how George might behave if the problem were removed, i.e. the miracle question idea. They are finally asked to identify three things that George could do now in order to remove the problem from his life.

Activity Sheets

Activity 1 – Drugs Awareness

In this activity the students are asked to look at the labels and to sort these into three categories as follows:

- Drugs that make us feel relaxed and sleepy.
- Drugs that make us imagine things.
- Drugs that make us feel energised.

The students are asked to discuss these in pairs, identifying which drugs do the most damage. They are then asked to rank these in order of danger from 1 to 13 and then share their ranking with the rest of the group.

Tip

The facilitator should take care when pairing students to ensure that within each group one student feels confident in recording and taking a lead.

Activity 2 – Drugs and the Law Quiz

In this activity students are asked to discuss a series of statements in pairs, identifying whether they are true or false. They are asked to circle the appropriate answer. The idea here is to clearly dispel any myths and ensure that students are aware of the consequences of any illegal behaviours. Answers have been provided on a separate sheet.

Plenary

The facilitator may wish to focus on the following questions:

- How much have we learnt about drugs in this session?
- What have we learnt about drugs and their relationship to the law in this session?
- How did we feel at the start of this session?
- How do we feel now at the end of this session?
- Do we think that the information presented in this session will change our behaviour in the future?

Tip

Make sure that this final question is not perceived, in any sense, as a judgement or a directive. If the students say that the information they've received won't change their behaviour, then simply acknowledge this and move on.

Drugs Awareness

Record all the words that you can think of below.

Drugs Awareness

Facilitator's Notes

Cannabis	Heroin
Cocaine	Cigarettes
Alcohol	Ecstasy
Skunk	Hallucinate
Sobriety	Abstinence
Abuse	Legal age
Paranoia	Peer pressure
Sick	Law
Safety	Risk taking

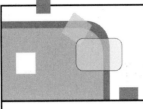

Quick Activity

Pair up with another person.
You have 2 minutes to agree on the 3 most popular
reasons for trying drugs. Be prepared to explain
your choice!

3 Most popular reasons for trying drugs
1.
2.
3.

Drugs Awareness

George has been friends with Keith and Bill for as long as he can remember but lately all they want to do is smoke cannabis. George has noticed that since they have been smoking on a daily basis, they are moody, they forget things, and they go on at him to join in. George will smoke with them occasionally but he really doesn't like it. He'd rather use his money on other things and he tends to get really paranoid when he takes it. Besides, he doesn't want to get schizophrenia, the thing the drugs teacher said they could get. The problem is that they are his only 'real' friends. Not only is he worried about their health but he doesn't really enjoy their company when they are stoned.

Notes

Solution-focused problem-solving format

How does **George** feel?

What is the problem?

How would **George** feel and behave if this problem disappeared?

How would **George** know that he would no longer have this problem? What would be different?

What 3 things can **George** do now in order to remove this problem from his life?

1)

2)

Drugs Awareness

There are many different types of drugs. They have different effects on us. Look at the labels below and sort them into the three sections of the circle.

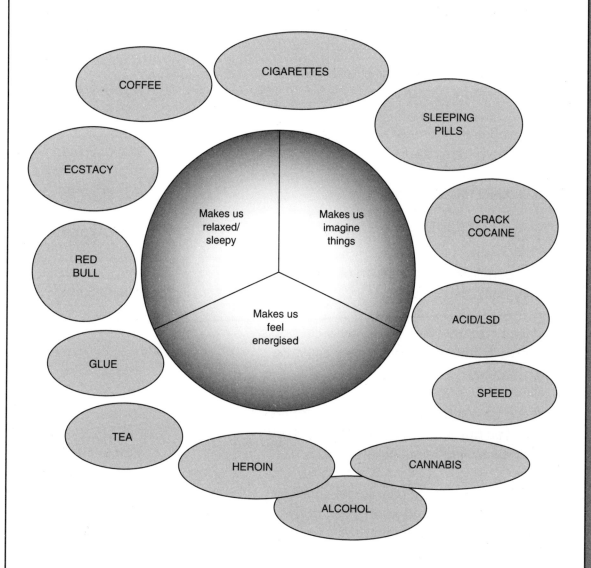

Discuss! In pairs discuss which drugs do the most damage. Put them in order of danger from 1 to 13. Share your ranking with the whole group.

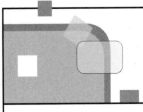

Drugs and the Law Quiz

Discuss in pairs whether the statements below are TRUE or FALSE. Circle the appropriate answer.

1. It is illegal to use steroids.   True or False

2. It is illegal to sell poppers (liquid gold) to someone under 16 years old.   True or False

3. It is illegal for two 14-year-olds to go into a pub without an adult.   True or False

4. It is illegal to pick magic mushrooms and take them home to dry out.   True or False

5. It is illegal to use a syringe.   True or False

6. Cocaine cannot be prescribed by a doctor.   True or False

7. The penalties for possession of cannabis vary from area to area.   True or False

8. If your parents allow you to grow cannabis plants in their greenhouse, they could be prosecuted.   True or False

9. If you go clubbing with two of your mates and you buy them ecstasy tablets, you can be prosecuted for supplying drugs.   True or False

10. It is illegal for you to offer to get some cannabis for a friend (even if you don't eventually manage to get any).   True or False

11. LSD is a class A drug (i.e. has the toughest penalties).   True or False

12. It is illegal for you to sniff aerosol in the street.   True or False

13. Heroin can be given by prescription.   True or False

14. The main law controlling drug use in the UK is called the Illegal Substances Act.   True or False

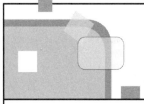

Drugs and the Law Quiz

Answer sheet

1. FALSE. They are only illegal if supplied or sold under the Medicines Act.

2. FALSE. There aren't any controls on poppers.

3. FALSE. 14-year-olds can go into a pub by themselves if the landlord agrees to it but they can't drink alcohol until they are 18 years old (16 years old if they have a meal).

4. TRUE. Eating raw magic mushrooms is not illegal. It is illegal to process them, dry them out or cook them.

5. FALSE. It is the use of the drugs and not the syringe itself which may be illegal.

6. FALSE. However, cocaine is hardly ever prescribed these days.

7. TRUE. It really depends on the courts and the police. In some areas small amounts found in possession may be ignored or you may be given a caution. In some other places you may get a fine or a criminal record.

8. TRUE. It is illegal to grow cannabis even if you don't use it and your parents would be held responsible.

9. TRUE. If you buy ecstasy, you can be charged.

10. TRUE. If the police manage to get evidence against you, then they can charge you for conspiracy to supply drugs.

11. TRUE, and so are heroin, cocaine and ecstasy.

12. FALSE.

13. TRUE. It is sometimes prescribed to terminally ill cancer patients as a painkiller. Addicts are more often given a methadone replacement which has similar properties to heroin.

14. FALSE. It is the Misuse of Drugs Act.

Introduction

Students are asked to focus on the following questions:

> When have you observed people being excluded or abused because they were different? What happened?
> What did you think and feel about this?

Students can record their views on the blank Key Words Brainstorm sheet provided, or the facilitator may wish to record students' views on a whiteboard or flip-chart.

Tip

The facilitator may wish to provide some initial examples to prompt thinking (see the Facilitator's Notes for some suggestions).

Brainstorm

Students are asked to brainstorm and to identify all the words and phrases that they can relate to this topic. The facilitator can once again provide initial prompts if necessary. Students can record their ideas on the blank Key Words Brainstorm sheet provided, or the facilitator may wish to scribe the students' responses on a whiteboard or flip-chart.

Quick Activity

Students are asked to work in pairs. The facilitator describes the task and explains to the students that this is a timed activity. They have two minutes to identify three famous people who have encouraged the world to be more tolerant of different types of people. Ideas can be recorded on the Quick Activity sheet provided. It may be helpful to provide students with the following example:

> Three famous people who have encouraged the world to be more tolerant of different types of people are:
>
> 1. Bob Geldof.
> 2. Bob Marley.
> 3. Martin Luther King.

Circle Talk

The group rules can once again be reinforced prior to engaging in the circle talk activity. This activity utilises the Circle Time approach and students can be asked to focus upon the following questions:

- What does the word 'tolerance' mean?
- How are people not tolerant within our society?
- What happens when people emotionally abuse or disrespect others?
- Have we ever experienced someone being abusive to us in this way?
- How did we cope with it?
- What did we do?
- How did we feel?
- Did anyone help us?

Problem Scenario

The students are presented with the problem scenario entitled 'Tolerance'. In this scenario Ahmed is feeling very upset both at his own behaviour towards his mum and at members of his peer group and their attitude towards her. His mother is very overweight and he resents her because of this fact. However, he also loves his mum and feels guilty about how embarrassed she makes him feel and how this often causes him to tease her. He wishes he could stop himself from being unkind towards her but isn't sure how he can break this pattern of behaviour.

The facilitator can read the problem scenario to the students. Alternatively, students may wish to read the text to themselves or nominate another student to read it aloud. They can then make use of the Solution-focused Problem-solving Format in order to identify a way forward for Ahmed. This involves identifying how Ahmed feels, clarifying the problem and how Ahmed might behave if the problem were removed, i.e. the miracle question idea. They are finally asked to identify three things that Ahmed could currently do in order to reach a state of 'life without the problem'.

Activity Sheets

Activity 1 – Tolerant or Not?

In this activity the students are asked to read a range of scenarios and discuss in the group a series of questions identifying who is and who is not being tolerant. They are asked to assess whether or not the main character should have behaved in this way and what they also think should or might happen next. In each of the scenarios students are behaving in an intolerant manner towards someone who is not in the position to be able to combat such intolerance or abuse.

Activity 2 – How Would You Feel If . . . ?

This is a self-reflection task in which students are asked to consider a range of statements and say how they would feel if they were in this particular position and why they would feel this way.

The statements include the following:

▸ You thought you might be gay.

▸ You were the only black student in your class.

▸ You couldn't walk and you were paralysed from the waist down.

▸ Your dad was gay.

▸ You didn't have nice clothes.

▸ You were really poor, etc.

The students are finally asked to identify three more situations in which they might have some difficulty or problem.

Tip

Be aware that for some young men it will not be possible at this stage even to discuss the possibility of being gay. This is fine. Acknowledge this fact without passing judgement and then move on.

Plenary

The facilitator may wish to focus on the following questions:

▸ What have we learnt about ourselves in this session?

▸ What have we learnt about our responses to others?

▸ Are we tolerant?

▸ Are others tolerant towards us in our community or school?

▸ How did we feel at the start of this session?

▸ How do we feel now at the end of this session?

- How would we combat the kinds of intolerance we have discussed in this session?

- What could be done?

- What could we do and what could others do?

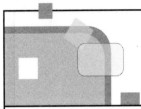

Key Words Brainstorm

Tolerance

Record all the words that you can think of below.

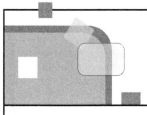

Tolerance

Facilitator's Notes

Equality	**Judge**
Value	**Acceptance**
Inclusion	**Exclusion**
Racist	**Sexist**
Homophobia	**Stereotype**
Understanding	**Difference**
Multicultural	**Social Justice**

Quick Activity

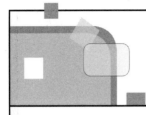

Pair up with another person.
You have 2 minutes to agree on 3 famous people who have encouraged the world to be more tolerant of different types of people.
Be prepared to explain your choice!

3 Famous people who have encouraged the world to be more tolerant of different types of people
1.
2.
3.

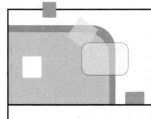

Tolerance

Ahmed's mum is really overweight. The kids at school have always teased him about her; used all the 'your mama' jokes you can think of. Ahmed can't help but resent his mum for her weight. He and his dad often joke and she usually ends up in tears. Ahmed knows he is hurting her but he won't stop himself. In the end, he feels guilty for upsetting her and vows not to do it again but it happens again the next day. Ahmed doesn't know how he can get himself out of this cycle. After all, it is his mum and he wants to accept her for who she is, not what she looks like.

Notes

Problem Scenario: Ahmed (Tolerance)

Solution-focused problem-solving format

How does **Ahmed** feel?

What is the problem?

How would **Ahmed** feel and behave if this problem disappeared?

How would **Ahmed** know that he would no longer have this problem? What would be different?

What 3 things can **Ahmed** do now in order to remove this problem from his life?

1)

2)

3)

Tolerant or not?

Stop!

Think!

Reflect!

Discuss!

Read the following scenarios and discuss in your group the following questions:

1. Who is not being tolerant?
2. Why do you think he/she/they behaved in this way?
3. What do you think should/might happen next?

Basil refuses to sit next to Ali because he says he is a smelly Paki and an illegal immigrant. DISCUSS.

Sara hasn't invited Alice to her party because she is fat. She doesn't want to be seen around ugly or fat girls as this might put the boys off her. DISCUSS.

Adam hasn't been chosen to swim in the relay race even though he's good at swimming. Adam is blind and partially deaf. DISCUSS.

Marja didn't get the Saturday job even though she performed the best in her interview. The owner felt her Muslim head wrap would put off customers. DISCUSS.

Marcus was not allowed to visit Tony because Tony's dad said he would not let wogs into his house. DISCUSS.

Jason was beaten up by six boys from Year 10. His face was smashed to a pulp and he's in intensive care. They said that he deserved it because he is a poof. DISCUSS.

How would you feel if...?

Self-reflection

Stop and think about each statement and then say how you would feel (and why) if …

- You thought you might be gay.

- You were the only black student in your class.

- You were mixed race.

- You couldn't walk and you were paralysed from the waist down.

- You were the only homosexual in the school.

- Your dad was gay.

- You didn't have nice clothes.

- You were really poor.

- You were really rich.

- Your sister had cerebral palsy.

- Your friend told you he/she was gay.

- No one spoke your language at school.

- You couldn't read or write as well as the other kids in your class.

- You didn't have any friends.

- You couldn't get through the day without a drink.

- You were the only person in your class who believed in God and practised your religion.

Can you think of three more?

-

-

-

Introduction

Students are asked to focus on the following questions:

> Why do people commit crimes?
> What are their motivations and reasons?

Students can record their views on the blank Key Words Brainstrom sheet provided, or the facilitator may wish to record students' views on a whiteboard or flip-chart.

> **Tip**
>
> **If necessary, the facilitator can model initial thoughts and responses here in order to prompt students' thinking (see the Facilitator's Notes for some suggestions).**

Brainstorm

Students are asked to brainstorm and to identify all the words and phrases that they can relate to this topic. The facilitator can once again provide initial prompts if necessary. Students can record their ideas on the blank Key Words Brainstorm sheet provided, or the facilitator may wish to scribe the students' responses on a whiteboard or flip-chart.

Quick Activity

Students are asked to work in pairs. The facilitator describes the task and explains to the students that this is a timed activity. They have two minutes to identify three reasons why young people commit crimes. Ideas can be recorded on the Quick Activity sheet provided. It may be helpful to provide students with the following example:

Three reasons why young people commit crimes are:

1. Boredom.
2. Being in a crew.
3. Frustration – you can't express your needs to anyone.

Circle Talk

The group rules can once again be reinforced prior to engaging in the circle talk activity. This activity utilises the Circle Time approach and students can be asked to focus upon the following questions:

▶ What is a crime?

▶ Are some crimes worse than others?

▶ How do we punish people who commit crimes in our society?

▶ Does punishment always work?

▶ Do people go on to re-offend if they have been institutionalised by the prison system?

▶ How can people be prevented from committing crimes?

▶ What needs to happen in order to stop people committing crimes?

▶ How could a crime-free society ever exist?

▶ What would need to happen?

Problem Scenario

The students are presented with the problem scenario entitled 'Crime and Punishment'. In this scenario, Chris has fallen into a pattern of offending behaviour, having frequently stolen from a range of local businesses. He has justified his behaviour to himself by saying that he is only stealing from those who are rich and not poor. However, he has recently stolen the rent money from his mother's purse and, consequently, he and his mum face an eviction notice.

The facilitator can read the problem scenario to the students. Alternatively, students may wish to read the text to themselves or nominate another student to read it aloud. They can then make use of the Solution-focused Problem-solving Format in order to identify a way forward for Chris. This involves identifying how Chris feels, clarifying the problem and how Chris might behave if the problem were removed, i.e. the miracle question idea. They are finally asked to identify three things that Chris could do now in order to remove the problem from his life.

Activity Sheets

Activity 1 – Crime and Punishment

In this activity the students are presented with a series of statements. These can be photocopied onto card beforehand and cut out at the start of the session. The students are asked to identify which is the worst crime and to sequence the crimes in order of seriousness, i.e. the most serious first and the least serious last. They are then asked to discuss their ranking process as a group and to also consider what punishment they think would be appropriate for each of the crimes listed.

Tip

If students are finding it difficult to cooperate or agree, then this activity can be completed individually. Highlight the fact that there is probably no 'right' way of ordering the crimes and that all their ideas are valid. What is important is that they can justify them.

Activity 2 – Crime Feelings

The students are asked to identify how the victim, the perpetrator and an observer might feel about a series of crimes presented on the worksheet. They are asked to discuss these with members of their family, i.e. this is a take-home task for students to do in the home context. Alternatively, if this is not possible, the students can complete the activity within the session.

Plenary

The facilitator may wish to focus on the following questions:

▸ What have we learnt about crime and punishment in this session?

▸ What do we consider to be the worst crime possible?

▸ Are some crimes ever justified?

▸ How did we feel at the start of this session?

▸ How do we feel now at the end of the session?

▸ What have we learnt about crime and punishment in this session that may be useful to us in the future?

Crime and punishment

Record all the words that you
can think of below

Crime and Punishment

Facilitator's Notes

Busted	Dealing
Youth Offending Team	Thief
Graffiti	Prison
Tag	Crime
Sentence	Shoplift
Law	Police
Copper	Judge
Court	

Quick Activity

Pair up with another person.
You have 2 minutes to agree on 3 reasons why young people commit crimes.
Be prepared to explain your choice!

3 Reasons why young people commit crimes
1.
2.
3.

Crime and Punishment

Chris steals stuff all the time. Chris tells his mates that it doesn't hurt anyone because the businesses have so much money they won't miss a couple of things here and there. Chris gets caught sometimes and when he does his mum has to come down to the station to bail him out. She usually breaks down crying and making a big scene. This time things are a bit different. Chris decides to steal the rent money out of his mum's purse. Chris's mum has been late on her payments for the last few months so when she doesn't give the landlord the money on time this month they receive an eviction notice.

Notes

Solution-focused problem-solving format

How does **Chris** feel?

What is the problem?

How would **Chris** feel and behave if this problem disappeared?

How would **Chris** know that he would no longer have this problem? What would be different?

What 3 things can **Chris** do now in order to remove this problem from his life?

1)

2)

3)

Crime and Punishment

Which is the 'worst' crime? Which is the least serious? Cut out and order the following crimes. Place the most serious first. Then discuss in a group which punishments would be appropriate for each crime.

'Graffiti' on the school building	Raping a girl	Dealing Smack
Sexually abusing an old person	Beating up an old lady	Cheating in an exam
Raping a boy	Taking heroin	Gang fighting
Knifing someone in a fight	Shoplifting	Arson
Stealing from someone's house	Bullying a younger boy	Sexually abusing a child
Mugging an older man	Stealing a car and joyriding	Stabbing someone because they are black
Stealing money from your mum's purse	Speeding in a car	Making malicious phone calls
Not paying your bus or train fare	Happy slapping	Drinking and driving

Crime Feelings

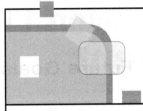

How would the victim, the perpetrator and the observer feel about the following crimes? STOP, THINK, AND TALK with members of your family and friends. Complete the chart below.

CRIME	Victim's feelings	Perpetrator's feelings	Observer's feelings
A girl is raped by an older boy			
An old man is mugged by a group of girls			
A boy steals a younger child's mobile phone			
A drug dealer gives some heroin to a 'new' younger user			
A woman is physically and verbally abused because she is Muslim and wearing a head covering			
A man steals a woman's car and crashes it into a lamp-post			

Session 11

Future Goals

Introduction

Students are asked to focus on the following questions:

> If you could do or be anything/anyone in the future, what would you do or who would you be? Why?

Students can record their views on the blank Key Words Brainstorm sheet provided, or the facilitator may wish to record students' views on a whiteboard or flip-chart.

Tip

The facilitator can join in here (see the Facilitator's Notes for some suggestions). This will help to prompt thinking and perhaps reduce any embarrassment, encouraging students to be imaginative and open.

Brainstorm

Students are asked to brainstorm and to identify all the words and phrases that they can relate to this topic. The facilitator may choose to model initial responses again. Ideas can be recorded on the blank Key Words Brainstorm sheet provided, or the facilitator may wish to scribe the students' suggestions on a whiteboard or flip-chart.

Quick Activity

Students are asked to work in pairs. The facilitator describes the task and explains to the students that this is a timed activity. They have two minutes to identify the three most important things that young people want in the future. Ideas can be recorded on the Quick Activity sheet provided. It may be helpful to provide students with the following example:

Three most important things that young people want in the future are:

1. Money.
2. A family.
3. A home.

Circle Talk

The group rules can once again be reinforced prior to engaging in the circle talk activity. This activity utilises the Circle Time approach and students can be asked to focus upon the following questions:

- How do we feel about the future?
- Are our feelings negative or positive?
- How can we remain motivated and envisage a positive future for ourselves?
- Who can help us in this process?
- How can we help ourselves?
- What would our dream futures be?

Problem Scenario

The students are presented with the problem scenario entitled 'Future Goals'. In this scenario Anthony is feeling very angry and rather stressed. He has always found academic work rather difficult. This led to teasing which in turn de-motivated him. Consequently, he has not achieved good grades but he has identified car mechanics as a possible future career route. He now wants to go to college to study mechanics but both school staff and his parents are saying that they will not support his application because he has not achieved good grades and has a bad attitude.

The facilitator can read the problem scenario to the students. Alternatively, students may wish to read the text to themselves or nominate another student to read it aloud. They can then make use of the Solution-focused Problem-solving Format in order to identify a way forward for Anthony. This involves identifying how Anthony feels, clarifying the problem and how Anthony might behave if the problem were removed, i.e. the miracle question idea. They are finally asked to identify three things that Anthony could do now in order to remove the problem from his life.

Activity Sheets

Activity 1 – My Preferred Future

In this activity students are asked to try and imagine themselves in ten years' time. Where would they like to be? How would they want to feel? What would they want to be doing?, etc. They are then asked to sketch their 'Ten Years Forward' portrait and record their ideas around the picture frame.

Activity 2 – My Future Goals

In this activity the students are asked to identify what they would need to do in order to achieve their preferred future. They are asked to set three 'SMART' targets (Specific, Measurable, Achievable, Realistic, Time-limited) and then to discuss these targets with a partner, identifying who else could help them reach their goals. When would they know that they had achieved each of their targets, i.e. what would be different, how would they feel and how would they act if this were the case?

Plenary

The facilitator may wish to focus on the following questions:

▸ What have we learnt about ourselves and our level of motivation?

▸ What have we learnt about each other during this session?

▸ How do we feel about our futures?

▸ How did we feel at the start of this session?

▸ How do we feel now at the end of this session?

▸ Will this session make a difference to our futures?

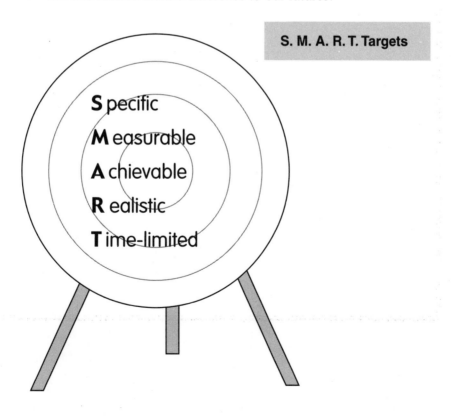

S. M. A. R. T. Targets

S pecific
M easurable
A chievable
R ealistic
T ime-limited

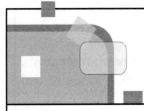

Future Goals

Record all the words that you can think of below.

Future Goals

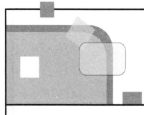

Facilitator's Notes

Dreams	**Vision**
Hopes	**Risk taking**
Careers	**Support systems**
Targets	**Self-belief**
Family	**Fears**
Goals	**Plans**
Future	

Quick Activity

Pair up with another person.
You have 2 minutes to agree on the 3 most important things
that young people want in the future.
Be prepared to explain your choice!

3 Most important things that young people want in the future
1.
2.
3.

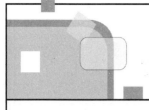

Future Goals

Anthony hates school. When he was in Year 7 he was teased by the other students because he got the lowest marks in an English test. Ever since, Anthony hasn't bothered trying. Teachers have tried to encourage him and so have his parents but they seem to have given up on him now. The only thing he likes and is good at is cars. Anthony's uncle has taught him lots about cars. Now that Anthony is in Year 10 he wants to get a college placement working in mechanics but the school and his parents say they won't let him because of his grades and his attitude.

Notes

Solution-focused problem-solving format

How does **Anthony** feel?

What is the problem?

How would **Anthony** feel and behave if this problem disappeared?

How would **Anthony** know that he would no longer have this problem? What would be different?

What 3 things can **Anthony** do now in order to remove this problem from his life?

1)

2)

3)

My Preferred Future

Try to imagine yourself in ten years' time. Where would you like to be? How would you want to feel? What would you want to be doing? Where would you want to live and work?

Sketch your 'Ten Years Forward' portrait and record your ideas around the picture frame.

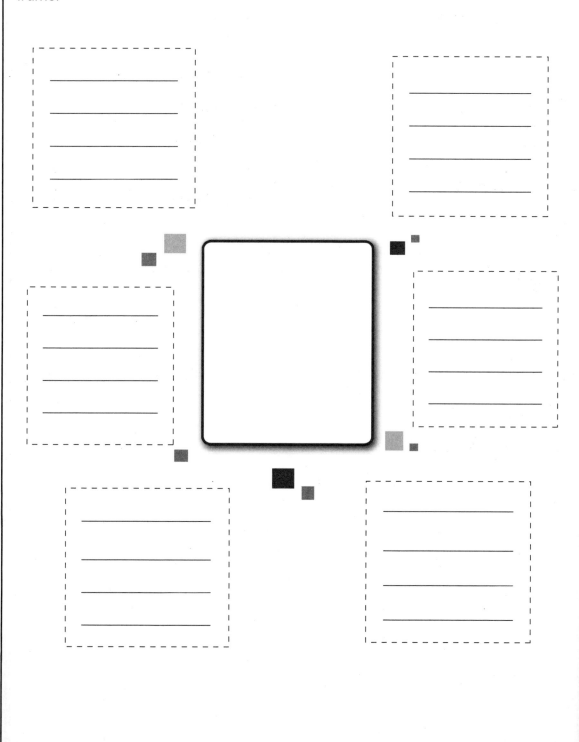

My Future Goals

What do you need to do in order to achieve your preferred future?

Set yourself some S. M. A. R. T. targets!

Target 1

Target 2

Target 3

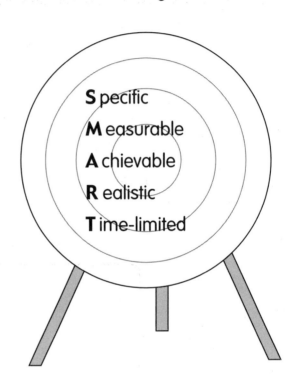

S pecific

M easurable

A chievable

R ealistic

T ime-limited

Discuss with a partner:

- Who else can help me achieve these goals?

- How will I know when I achieve each of these targets?

- What will be different?

- How will I feel?

- How will I act?

Evaluation

Introduction

Students are asked to focus on the following questions:

>   Why did we do in this course?
>   What do you think was the main objective?

Students can record their views on the blank Key Words Brainstorm sheet provided or the facilitator may wish to record students' views on a whiteboard or flip-chart.

Tip

The facilitator can provide some initial ideas to prompt thinking and responses (see the Facilitator's Notes for some suggestions).

Brainstorm

Students are asked to brainstorm and to identify all the words and phrases that they can relate to this topic. The facilitator can once again provide initial prompts if necessary. Students can record their ideas on the blank Key Words Brainstorm sheet provided, or the facilitator may wish to scribe the students' responses on a whiteboard or flip-chart.

Quick Activity

Students are asked to work in pairs. The facilitator describes the task and explains to the students that this is a timed activity. They have two minutes to identify the three most important things that all boys should learn before they become an adult. Ideas can be recorded on the Quick Activity sheet provided. It may be helpful to provide students with the following example:

Three most important things that all boys should learn before they become an adult are:

1. Respect for self and others.
2. The value of hard work.
3. The law.

Circle Talk

The group rules can once again be reinforced prior to engaging in the circle talk activity. This activity utilises the Circle Time approach and students can be asked to focus upon the following questions:

▸ How do we feel about the things that we have covered in this course?

▸ Do we feel any different?

▸ Do we feel the same?

▸ Do we feel that our knowledge has increased about the topics that we have covered?

▸ Do we feel that we could be better friends and more able to keep safe in social situations?

▸ Do we feel more able to talk about how we feel?

▸ Do we feel more able to empathise with and tolerate others?

▸ Are we more confident about our futures?

Problem Scenario

The students are presented with the problem scenario entitled 'Evaluation'. In this scenario Ryan has just left a Pupil Referral Unit and transferred back to mainstream school. He was able to modify his behaviours and experience success at the unit but this is put in jeopardy on his first day at his new school. He meets his first teacher who immediately makes it clear that Ryan has already been labelled as a troublemaker and is not wanted in the school.

The facilitator can read the problem scenario to the students. Alternatively, students may wish to read the text to themselves or nominate another student to read it aloud. They can then make use of the Solution-focused Problem-solving Format in order to identify a way forward for Ryan. This involves identifying how Ryan feels, clarifying the problem and how Ryan might behave if the problem were removed, i.e. the miracle question idea. They are finally asked to identify three things that Ryan could do now in order to remove the problem from his life.

Activity Sheets

Activity 1 – Brainstorming Activity

In this activity the students are asked to brainstorm the question 'What have we learnt in this course?' The facilitator can prompt the students in this activity as appropriate.

It may be helpful to refer back to the flip-chart utilised in the first session where course objectives and the course content were outlined.

Tip

Take the stress out of recording by acting as a scribe for the students' responses.

Activity 2 – Evaluation of Boys' World

In this two-part activity the students are asked to rate themselves on a scale of 1–10 (1 = not good, 5 = OK, 10 = excellent) for how well they think they have developed their skills in a series of key areas. These include self-esteem, confidence, coping with peer pressure, knowledge of sex, HIV and AIDS, their ability to talk about feelings, etc. The students are then asked to evaluate the course activities using the same scale and to provide some feedback for the facilitators, identifying what they would change in order to make the course better for future groups of students.

Tip

Encourage the students to be honest in their self-assessment and highlight the importance of their views. If they have not enjoyed the course, or some aspects of it, then now is their time to say so. Explain that without their feedback you cannot change what you do and make it better or more relevant for other groups of boys.

Certificate of Achievement

The final worksheet takes the form of a Certificate of Achievement. These can be awarded to students in this session or alternatively the facilitator may wish to organise a special presentation within an assembly context. The Certificates will need to be copied onto card and laminated as appropriate.

Plenary

The facilitator may wish to focus on the following questions:

▸ What have we learnt about ourselves in this course?

▸ What have we learnt about other people in this course?

▸ How did we feel at the start of this course?

▸ How do we feel now at the end of this course?

Tip

The facilitator needs to join in here. Modelling responses and giving the group a sense of what you have learnt and how you feel about it all will be important in terms of ensuring a real sense of democracy and working together.

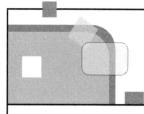

Evaluation

Record all the words that you can think of below.

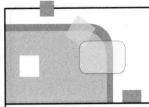

Evaluation

Facilitator's Notes

Useful	**Unhelpful**
Positive	**Engaging**
Negative	**Beliefs**
Good	**Values**
Bad	**Enjoyable**
Boring	**Learning experience**
Helpful	**Likes/Dislikes**
Achievements	**Reflection**

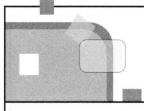

Quick Activity

Pair up with another person.
You have 2 minutes to agree on the 3 most
important things that all boys should learn before
they become an adult
Be prepared to explain your choice!

1.

2.

3.

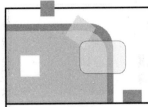

Evaluation

Ryan was excluded from school six months ago. At first he was angry at everyone. Then he started to realise that if he stopped blaming everyone else and tried harder, he could make something of himself. He was temporarily placed in a Pupil Referral Unit. He then listened to the teachers, did his work, made a lot of mistakes, but gained the respect of the teachers, his parents and most importantly himself. All was looking great until he started his first day at a new school and the first teacher he met said to him, 'So you are the troublemaker we were forced to take. You better watch yourself because we do not tolerate bad behaviour in this school.'

Notes

Solution-focused problem-solving format

How does **Ryan** feel?

What is the problem?

How would **Ryan** feel and behave if this problem disappeared?

How would **Ryan** know that he would no longer have this problem? What would be different?

What 3 things can **Ryan** do now in order remove this problem from his life?

1)

2)

3)

Brainstorming Activity

What have we learnt
in Boys' World?

Evaluation of Boys' World

Looking at You!

Rate yourself on a scale of 1–10 (1 = not good, 5 = OK, 10 = excellent) for how well you think you have developed your skills in each of the following areas. Please circle your choice.

Not Good   **OK**   **Excellent**

Your level of self-esteem

1   2   3   4   5   6   7   8   9   10

Your level of confidence

1   2   3   4   5   6   7   8   9   10

Your ability to cope with peer pressure

1   2   3   4   5   6   7   8   9   10

Your knowledge of sex, HIV and AIDS

1   2   3   4   5   6   7   8   9   10

Your knowledge of safe sex

1   2   3   4   5   6   7   8   9   10

Evaluation of Boys' World

Not Good   **OK**   **Excellent**

Your ability to mediate and solve problems

1   2   3   4   5   6   7   8   9   10

Your ability to recognise and talk about your feelings

1   2   3   4   5   6   7   8   9   10

Your knowledge of drugs and substance abuse and the laws on drugs

1   2   3   4   5   6   7   8   9   10

Your ability to tolerate difference (e.g. race, sexuality)

1   2   3   4   5   6   7   8   9   10

Your understanding of offending behaviours and how these impact upon others

1   2   3   4   5   6   7   8   9   10

Your ability to think positively and set realistic targets

1   2   3   4   5   6   7   8   9   10

Your ability to empathise with others

1   2   3   4   5   6   7   8   9   10

Evaluation of Boys' World

Looking at the Course Activities

Use the same scale (1 = not good, 5 = OK, 10 = excellent) to rate the following activities.

Brainstorming activities

1   2   3   4   5   6   7   8   9   10

Quick activities

1   2   3   4   5   6   7   8   9   10

Circle talk

1   2   3   4   5   6   7   8   9   10

Problem scenarios

1   2   3   4   5   6   7   8   9   10

Activity sheets

1   2   3   4   5   6   7   8   9   10

Plenary

1   2   3   4   5   6   7   8   9   10

What did you enjoy the most? Why?

What did you enjoy the least? Why?

If we ran the course again, what advice would you give to us in order to make it better?

Thank you for your help and advice!

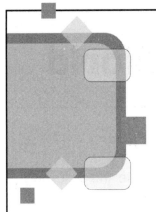

Certificate
of
Achievement

This certificate is awarded to

in recognition of valuable contributions

to Boys' World.

CONGRATULATIONS!

Signature

Date

Signature

Date